ZEN CHANTS

Zen Chants

Thirty-Five Essential Texts
with Commentary

Kazuaki Tanahashi

PHOTOGRAPHY BY MITSUE NAGASE

SHAMBHALA
BOSTON & LONDON
2015

Shambhala Publications, Inc.
Horticultural Hall
300 Massachusetts Avenue
Boston, MA 02115
www.shambhala.com

9 8 7 6 5 4 3 2 1

First Edition
Printed in the United States of America

♾ This edition is printed on acid-free paper that meets the
American National Standards Institute Z39.48 Standard.
♻ This book is printed on 30% postconsumer recycled paper.
For more information please visit www.shambhala.com.

Distributed in the United States by Penguin Random House LLC
and in Canada by Random House of Canada Ltd

Designed by Gopa & Ted2, Inc.

Library of Congress Cataloging-in-Publication Data

Tanahashi, Kazuaki, 1933– author.
Zen chants: thirty-five essential texts with commentary /
Kazuaki Tanahashi; photography by Mitsue Nagase.—
First edition.
pages   cm
Includes bibliographical references.
ISBN 978-1-61180-143-9 (pbk.: alk. paper)
1. Zen Buddhism—Prayers and devotions. I. Nagase, Mitsue. II. Title.
BQ9287.4.T36 2015
294.3'438—dc23
2014033961

To Sojun Mel Weitsman
with smiles and bows

Contents

Illustrations   xi

Preface and Acknowledgments   1

Introduction   7

Notes to the Reader   23

PART ONE. DAILY CHANTS

    Awakening Together   29

    Four All-Embracing Vows   30

    Ten-Line Life-Affirming Sūtra of Avalokiteshvara   31

    Sūtra on the Heart of Realizing Wisdom Beyond Wisdom   32

    Meal Chant   34

    Robe Verse   35

    Three Refuges   36

    Mettā   37

    Great Compassionate Heart Dhāraṇī   38

    Wondrous Auspicious Dhāraṇī
for Averting Calamities   39

    Dedication   40

    Buddha Ancestors   41

    Female Buddha Ancestors   44

    Atonement   47

    Reminder   48

Part Two. Chants for Events

Opening the Sūtra Verse   51
Verse for Hearing the Mallet   52
Setting Out the Bowls   53
Invocation   55
Offering Food for Spirits   56
Raising the Bowl   57
Offering Rinse Water   58
Verse of Pure Practice   59
Universal Precepts of the Seven Original Buddhas   60
Maintaining the Precepts   61
Admonition   62

Part Three. Enlightenment Poems

Engraving Trust in the Heart   67
Song of Realizing the Way   73
Being One and Many   85
Song of the Grass Hut   88
The Jewel Mirror Awareness   90
The Point of Zazen   95
In Praise of Zazen   96

Part Four. Prose Chants for Study

Recommending Zazen to All People   101
On the Endeavor of the Way   105
Actualizing the Fundamental Point   111

PART FIVE. THE TEXTS ILLUMINATED

Daily Chants   119

    Awakening Together   119

    Four All-Embracing Vows   121

    Ten-Line Life-Affirming Sūtra of Avalokiteshvara   123

    Sūtra on the Heart of Realizing
    Wisdom Beyond Wisdom   126

    Meal Chant   130

    Robe Verse   132

    Three Refuges   134

    Mettā   135

    Great Compassionate Heart Dhāranī   136

    Wondrous Auspicious Dhāranī for
    Averting Calamities   140

    Dedication   142

    Buddha Ancestors   143

    Female Buddha Ancestors   144

    Atonement   145

    Reminder   147

Chants for Events   149

    Opening the Sūtra Verse   149

    Verse for Hearing the Mallet   150

    Setting Out the Bowls   152

    Invocation   153

    Offering Food for Spirits   155

    Raising the Bowl   156

    Offering Rinse Water   157

Verse of Pure Practice   159

Universal Precepts of the Seven Original Buddhas   160

Maintaining the Precepts   161

Admonition   162

Enlightenment Poems   165

Engraving Trust in the Heart   165

Song of Realizing the Way   167

Being One and Many   174

Song of the Grass Hut   176

Song of the Jewel Mirror Awareness   176

The Point of Zazen   179

In Praise of Zazen   180

Prose Chants for Study   183

Recommending Zazen to All People   183

On the Endeavor of the Way   183

Actualizing the Fundamental Point   186

Notes   187

Selected Bibliography   189

ILLUSTRATIONS

p. 5:   Sounding the *han* to signal meditation. Ho Sen Dojo, Antwerp, Belgium.

p. 25:   Zendo in early morning. Tassajara Zen Mountain Center, Carmel Valley, California.

p. 28:   Chanting before the dharma talk. Berkeley Zen Center, Berkeley, California.

p. 50:   Bowing with wrapped *oryoki* bowls. Ho Sen Dojo, Antwerp, Belgium.

p. 54:   Chanting at priest ordination ceremony. Upaya Zen Center, Santa Fe, New Mexico.

p. 66:   Chanting before trekking. Nomads Clinic in northwestern Nepal, organized by Upaya Zen Center.

p. 100: Chanting before *samu* (work) period. Tassajara Zen Mountain Center, Carmel Valley, California.

p. 118: Nuns singing. Plum Village Monastery, Loubès-Bernac, France.

Preface and Acknowledgments

THE RECITATION OF CHANTS—both during a meditation gathering and outside of it—represents the aspiration, vows, realization, and commitments of Zen practitioners. Some chants are recited daily, while others are used only for special occasions. The recitation process helps to shape, confirm, and expand your meditation experience and mindfulness practice. Thus, by familiarizing yourself with Zen chants, you access the spirit of Zen and gain insight.

The landscape of Zen practice fills monasteries, Buddhist centers, and Zen gatherings. Beyond such settings, meditation can be conducted almost anywhere—at home, in a hospital, in nature, on an airplane or boat, or in a train station. In reality, it can be done anywhere on the globe. Mitsue Nagase's photography in this book suggests diverse settings for meditation and chanting—in sitting postures, walking meditation, ceremonies, services, as well as during mindful working, eating, and other meditation-based daily activities—in a variety of places in the United States, Europe, and Asia.

It is my great pleasure to present a selection of translations recited in English-speaking countries. In these regions, Chan or Zen groups, whose traditions originate in China, Korea, Japan, and Vietnam, commonly recite some of these chants in a variety of translations. Some of the verses were recited originally in Sanskrit, and many in Chinese. Other texts derive from Japan and are recited only by groups of Japanese origin, such as the Soto and Rinzai schools.

I have arranged the materials as a text that is interesting for reading, instead of in the usual chanting order. Chants in this book are divided into four parts: "Daily Chants," "Chants for Events," "Enlightenment Poems," and "Chants for Study." However, this classification is rather arbitrary. In monasteries and Zen centers, some of the chants classified otherwise may be chanted daily. In small groups, those that are classified here as daily chants may be chanted only during special events.

Many of the Zen groups I am associated with have been established by teachers from Japan, so they chant some versions in Japanese. That explains my choice of texts and transliterations in Japanese. Regrettably, I have been unable to find female teachers' enlightenment poems for chanting or study. Thus, the texts I present in this book were all written by male teachers. Some American groups have begun chanting the names of female buddha ancestors; I am including one such chant here, hoping to address the imbalance in gender in our heritage.

Zen has a history of about fifteen hundred years, but some of the Buddhist chants presented here emerged over two thousand years ago. The newest chant I am including, other than the names of female buddha ancestors, is from the eighteenth century. Numberless Zen practitioners have engaged in the process of finding, selecting, and maintaining the originals of what we chant now. This book responds to a need for a collection/book of chants that is easy to understand, fluid for chanting, and relevant to contemporary Western values.

For over thirty years, I have been translating Zen chants with outstanding collaborators. These translations are inspired by a great variety of recitations I participated in while visiting dharma centers of different traditions in North America and Europe, where I teach East Asian calligraphy and at times give dharma talks.

I fully understand if you prefer to stay with the versions you have been chanting for years. Still, I encourage you and your group to use this book as a reference—both to reexamine chants you know and love, and to create new versions of the chants. You may also enjoy learning about the history of the chants outlined in the "Texts Illuminated" part of this book.

As most of the texts included in this book are derived from China, I present the Chinese ideographic versions of them in the "Texts Illuminated" part. You may not be familiar with ideographs, and they may have no meaning for you. However, just in case you are curious about original expressions, they are there. In the introduction, I will explain how to find online the meanings, pronunciations, and etymology of an ideograph. With this method, and without knowledge of an East Asian language, any of you can explore the world of ideography with great ease.

Because I designed this volume to serve as your final source book, so that you won't have to look for other books for your study, I am using macrons indicating long vowels in the main text. But the distinction between long and short vowels does not matter so much in English; macrons can be omitted for further use.

My first gratitude goes to countless practitioners of Chan and Zen all over East Asia, who have kept chanting these verses over a millennium and a half. The stunning insights of ancient Chinese and Japanese masters are still inspiring. The scholarship of commentators on these texts helps us to clarify their meanings.

Joan Halifax Roshi has been a wonderful cotranslator of many of the chanting texts. I thank Mel Weitsman Roshi, Jan Chozen Bays Roshi, Dr. Taigen Dan Leighton, Tom Cabarga, and the late Philip Whalen Roshi for their collaboration in translation. Peter Levitt, also a cotranslator, has provided me with very detailed comments on the texts throughout the book. Thanks to Dr. Susan O'Leary and my wife, Dr. Linda Hess, for their editorial advice. I owe much to the scholarship of Dr. Griffith Foulk on the Soto Zen liturgy. My appreciation for the research and editing goes to Rev. Roberta Werdinger. Also, thanks to Grace Schireson Roshi, Hogen Bays

Roshi, Dr. Szevone Chin, Zen Master Dae Gak, Mahiru Watanabe, Rev. Meg Gawler, Dr. Dieter Plempe, Simon Wiles, and Dr. Mary-Ray Cate for their help. Thanks to Mitsue Nagase for her photographs.

I thank Dr. Victor Hori, Andy Ferguson, Eri Suzuki, and Dawn Neal for their expertise and help. Thanks to Cheryl Kahn for the cover painting, Liza Matthews for cover design, and Gopa & Ted2, Inc., for the book design.

My gratitude goes to those who participated in creating the audio file of Selected Zen Chants: Gengo Akiba Roshi; residents of Upaya Zen Center, incuding Joshin Brian Byrnes, Genzan Quannell, and Andrew White; members of Salt Spring Zen Circle, Peter Levitt, Bill Henderson; Jiyu Caroline Savage, Sherry Shinge Chayat Roshi; Ensemble Polyfoon, Luc DeWinter; Metta Forest Monastery, Thanissaro Bhikku; Grace Schireson Roshi; and Karuna Tanahashi.

It's my pleasure again to work with Shambhala Publications staff, including Nikko Odiseos, Hazel Bercholz, and Ben Gleason. My special thanks to Dave O'Neal, who guided me through all stages of production, including copyediting.

—Kazuaki Tanahashi

Introduction

RECITATION HAS A major role in Zen life, with chanting taking place during services as well as at meals and other activities. Texts for chanting include prayers, scriptures, poems, essays, and admonitions.

In contrast to *zazen* (meditation in a sitting posture), walking meditation, and contemplative work, all of which are conducted with inward mindfulness in silence, chanting is expressed vocally, prompted by a leader, and often accompanied by bells and drums. Joining the palms together, bowing with the upper body or in full prostration, the chanters alternate between motion and stillness. Chanting can be done in temples or at home, in groups or individually. By and large, however, it is a communal activity.

Zen means "meditation." It is the Japanese transliteration of the Chinese word *chan,* which originally comes from the Sanskrit word for meditation, *dhyana. Zen* also refers to the larger Zen spiritual tradition—its practice, aesthetic, philosophy, and way of life. There are many reasons why people like to practice Zen. I find one of the best reasons for doing it in D. T. Suzuki's characterization of Zen as "a quiet, self-confident, and trustful existence of your own—this is the truth of Zen and what I mean when I say Zen is preeminently practical."[1]

Zen meditation is profoundly nourishing and enjoyable. At times, however, it is physically and psychologically challenging. Meditation can open us to much of the suffering of human existence, which can be extremely painful. Chanting together in full voice, with everyone's mind and heart pointed outward, is a dynamic, energizing activity that encourages us in our commitment and dedication to practice.

But the practice doesn't stop with chanting aloud with others. The recited texts can also be repeated in stillness and silence, reminding us of our understanding, vow, and commitment. Thus, Zen chants shape our meditation, consciousness, and life activities.

Reminders for an Awakened Life

The first three chants of this book present the concept of a *bodhisattva,* which means "one who helps others to awaken" or "enlightenment being." It was in Mahayana Buddhism, which originated some centuries after the lifetime of Shakyamuni Buddha, that the ideal of the bodhisattva developed. A bodhisattva is one who is willing to be the last one to be liberated in order to assist others in their awakening.

The difference between a *buddha*—which means an "awakened one"—and a *bodhisattva* ("one who helps others to awaken") may be perplexing for those who are not familiar with Buddhist terminology. But these two types of practitioners may not be mutually exclusive. We can be buddhas while we are awakened and be bodhisattvas while helping others.

To become a buddha is not a one-time achievement but a continuous process of becoming and remaining awakened. It is a dynamic, ongoing daily process. And yet, there is no perfectly awakened life without faults. We keep making mistakes and, unintentionally, harming others. Also, we are all products of the past violent or ignorant actions of individuals and society. That is our human condition. So we need to keep atoning together; the Verse of Atonement serves this purpose.

The "Four All-Embracing Vows" expresses the bodhisattva's attitude. The first of the four vows—"Beings are numberless; I vow to awaken them"—appears to be an overly idealistic and unrealistic promise. But if we look at it closely, we will notice that it doesn't simply say, "I vow to awaken all sentient beings." It begins by acknowledging just how many living beings there are who need to be awakened. Thus, being kind to a neighbor, a stranger, or an animal can create rippling effects of kindness. A simple action may cause infinite results. If the "I" who vows is separate from other people, what "I" can achieve is quite limited. But if "I" is not separate from all others throughout space and time, it may be possible to awaken all beings. This understanding is an essential ground for socially engaged Buddhism.

The Twofold Manifestation of Dharma

Loving-kindness is not simply a concept or feeling; it is a continuous commitment. We are all imperfect and often confused. We need a model for loving-kindness. As the most prominent personification of loving-kindness, Avalokiteshvara provides a perfect model for this quality. Thus, I feel the *Ten-Line Life-Affirming Sutra of Avalokiteshvara* can be a very useful chant for all dharma practitioners. It reminds us to be one with loving-kindness itself, realizing that the heart of loving-kindness rises and remains moment by moment.

Avalokiteshvara is also the main figure in the *Heart Sutra*—the sutra on "wisdom beyond wisdom." The fact that the personification of loving-kindness has such a prominent place in this sutra implies that loving-kindness and wisdom beyond wisdom are inseparable. They are together the essential manifestations of a mindful life.

"Wisdom beyond wisdom"—a translation of the Sanskrit word *prajna*—is different from conventional wisdom, which distinguishes good from bad and right from wrong. Prajna is the insight that transcends differences and sees that everything is undivided, without boundary. It is the wisdom of oneness.

This wisdom sees all phenomena as *shunyata*. *Shunyata,* the Sanskrit word usually translated as "emptiness," can also be interpreted as "zeroness." *Zero* primarily means "nothing," but it works like magic in mathematics, science, and engineering. *Shunyata* is translated as *kong* in Chinese and *ku* in Japanese, both meaning "sky." The sky may look empty, but in fact it encompasses all things, including the earth with us living on it. To acknowledge the all-inclusive meaning of this word, Joan Halifax and I have translated *shunyata* as "boundlessness," in our version of the *Heart Sutra.*

"Wisdom beyond wisdom" calls for going beyond the boundaries of large and small, right and wrong, self and other, momentariness and timelessness, and even life and death. It is this wisdom that helps us transcend the confinement of self and self-interest, allowing us to live more expansively. This is freedom from the illusion that we are the center of the universe and that our interests are the most important ones. It is freedom that can be experienced in meditation. No wonder the *Heart Sutra* is the most frequently chanted scripture on occasions of communal meditation practice in the Mahayana world.

You may feel that the *Heart Sutra* emphasizes only the erasure of dualistic views. But if you read it carefully, you'll see that it mentions freedom from nondualistic experiences as well. (For example, it says, "Boundlessness is free of old age and death, *and* free of the end of old age and death.") Thus, the *Heart Sutra* must be viewed as encouraging the transcendence of dualism or pluralism as well as of nondualism or singularism.

On one hand, we need pluralism to be able to conduct even the simplest tasks in life, such as distinguishing a dime from a quarter, getting somewhere on time, or functioning socially. In this regard, conventional pluralistic wisdom is necessary. On the other hand, we need singularism to see that all people and all elements of life are ultimately one. Pluralism and singularism both reflect reality; neither is more prominent than the other. Pluralism or singularism alone, however, limits our views and actions. From moment to moment in our everyday lives, we need perspectives with both kinds of wisdom—conventional wisdom and wisdom beyond wisdom. In fact, wisdom beyond wisdom should be inclusive of conventional wisdom.

Our life may be seen as a dance in which one foot represents pluralism and the other singularism. At any given moment, one foot touches the ground. The next moment, we use both. The moment after that, the other foot is on the ground by itself. If there is a slight misstep, we wobble. If we step stiffly, we become rigid. Each step is a challenge.

Can we see our dance in life and meditation as something other than switching between these seeming opposites? When the dancing flows naturally, singularism and pluralism are no longer in opposition. The opposites merge, allowing us to dance freely and gracefully. This is the manifestation of wisdom beyond wisdom, which is a wholesome experience of freedom from and integrity in pluralistic and singularistic understanding and action.

One Mind, One Heart

Zen chants are constant reminders that we practice together; we are one mind, one heart, one life. Even if we live or meditate alone, we are united with other awakened ones—not only with those in our immediate vicinity, but with all awakened beings from the past, present, and future, everywhere in the world.

The first chant in this book concludes with the line "Together may we realize wisdom beyond wisdom!" When we experience a sense of oneness with other individuals near and far, as well as with other living and nonliving beings, we are drawn toward selfless and compassionate states of mind. This may help us to make peace within ourselves, with our neighbors, and with our environment.

In his essay "Continuous Practice," the Zen master Dogen explains:

> By the continuous practice of all buddhas and ancestors, your practice is actualized and your great road opens up. By your continuous practice, the continuous practice of all buddhas is actualized and the great road of all buddhas opens up. Your continuous practice creates the circle of the way.[2]

When seen as a whole, Zen chants call for a concerted action by practitioners while meditating, taking refuge, making offerings, invoking buddhas, praying, thanking, reflecting, atoning, realizing, remembering the rarity and brevity of life, and becoming free. They always call for selfless consideration and for a willingness to assist others in need.

The phrasing in Zen recitation is pure, lofty, and solemn. But the chants can seem to be missing prayers for one's own health and happiness. We are all inseparable, and yet, each one of us is an individual human being who wants to be healthy and happy. In this regard, the "Metta," in Pali, provides an opportunity for us to pray for our own well-being and happiness as well as for that of others. It helps us to maintain a good balance between selflessness and happiness of the self.

Ambigu-theism

In some religions, there seems to be a clear-cut distinction between monotheism and polytheism. However, Buddhism—somewhat similar to Hinduism in this regard—is more complex and does not fit easily into either of these categories.

In a common Zen invocation, Vairochana Buddha—the pantheistic divinity regarded as existent in each and every particle—is addressed. Noting the presence of many buddhas and bodhisattvas in Zen, some of us may see it as polytheistic. Others regard Zen as atheistic, since the central figure on the altar is usually Shakyamuni Buddha—a human being, not a deity. Those who have faith in Amitabha Buddha often refuse to worship other divinities, so their practice may appear to fall into the category of monotheism.

Thus, Buddhists—including Zen practitioners—can be seen as running the gamut from having faith in a single deity to many deities to omnipresent deities to no deity at all. The ambiguity and diversity of this situation do not seem to bother people much. Accordingly, I propose a concept of *ambigu-theism* to characterize the theological orientation of Buddhism.

There is one common practice, however, for all Buddhists regardless of their belief or disbelief in God or deities. That is taking refuge in the three treasures—Buddha, dharma, and sangha. Buddha is an awakened one, whoever that awakened one might be taken to be. Dharma is the truth or teaching expounded by the Buddha. Sangha is a community that practices dharma, whether it is an intimate group of practitioners, a congregation, or practitioners throughout time all over the globe and beyond.

Paradox, Paradox, Paradox

The five Chinese and two Japanese verses included in the "Enlightenment Poems" part of this book point to meditators' dynamic experiences of realization and of the paradox inherent in the expression of that realization. One of the characteristics that distinguishes Zen from other schools of Buddhism is its partiality to paradox. Zen masters love to say things in a way that is enigmatic, nonlogical, and paradoxical. A sampling of such statements could include: Extremely small is large. Extremely large is small. Thinking is beyond thinking. Life is beyond life. Momentary is timeless. What is ultimately difficult is easy. What is obvious is profound. The path is the goal. Object is within subject. Host is within host. Not enlightened is enlightened. A bird flies like a bird. One is not separate from oneself. Not particular is extraordinary. Within nothing there is unlimitedness.

"Engraving Trust in the Heart" is full of paradox. Although it is attributed to Sengcan, the Third Chinese Ancestor, who lived in seventh-century China, it is difficult to imagine that a text in such a sophisticated style was written so early in the history of Zen. I am curious to know when the text was actually created.

Original Texts

Most Zen chants were first written in ideographs of Chinese origin. The Chan/Zen School of Buddhism started around the sixth century C.E. and developed in China before spreading to other parts of East Asia. Buddhists in this region use the same ideographs for chanting texts but pronounce them differently according to their particular linguistic systems.

For example, the ideographic version of the beginning of the *Heart Sutra,* "Avalokiteshvara, who helps all to awaken, moves in the deep course of realizing wisdom beyond wisdom" is

觀自在菩薩行深般若波羅蜜多時

This is pronounced as follows in the four languages below:

guan zi zai pu sa xing shen bo re bo luo mi duo shi (Chinese)

gwan ja jae bo sal haeng sim ban ya ba ra mil da si (Korean)
kan ji zai bo sa gyō jin han nya ha ra mit ta ji (Japanese)
quán tự tại bồ yát hành thâm bát nhã ba la mật đa thời
(Vietnamese)

Thus, the ideographic Chinese versions of the chants are invaluable sources for study and reference. In the "Texts Illuminated" part of this book, I present many of the ideographic versions of the texts. For some of you, ideographs may not be of particular interest or use. But just in case you would like to look for the original terms or phrases, they are right there. Nowadays, without knowing any East Asian languages, you can find ideographs and examine their meanings and usages through the Internet.[3]

Many of the Zen groups with which I am familiar in North America and Europe are in the lineage of Japanese Zen because their founding masters brought Zen teaching to these continents from Japan. These groups recite their main chanting texts in Sino-Japanese as well as in English.

There are at least two ways of reading an ideograph in Japanese. For example, the ideograph 山, meaning "mountain," is read *shan* in Chinese and *san* in Sino-Japanese. The other way of reading the same ideograph is to use an indigenous Japanese sound for the same meaning—*yama,* which the Japanese used before the ideographic system was introduced. You will also find in this book some Japanese Zen texts, including ones by Dogen, Myocho, and Hakuin, written in a mixture of ideographs and phonetics called kana.

Some chants include Sanskrit sounds. For example, the *Heart Sutra* concludes with a mantra, a kind of Sanskrit incantation that originated from ancient Vedic practice in India. Mantras used in Vajrayana Buddhism do not follow the rules of classical Sanskrit. They are often regarded as beyond meaning and therefore not translatable, though they are sometimes interpreted. A similar kind of Sanskrit chant is the *dharani*. It is also considered a mystic verse and is often longer than a mantra.

Some Pali chants have been recently included in Zen centers in the Western world. The Pali language is used in the South Asian and non-Mahayana traditions of Buddhism, which often reflect earlier Buddhist teachings than the Mahayana. The use of Pali chants reflects the inclusive and nonsectarian tendency of Buddhist practitioners in the West.

Translation and Adaptation

Many of the chants in English currently recited in Western Zen groups date back to the 1950s and 1960s when Zen practice first took shape in the Western world and ritual texts began to be translated. At that time, Buddhist language was just developing in North America and Europe. It is not surprising that some of these chants now sound awkward or that they have been discovered to be inaccurate. Many groups have made improvements and adaptations of these early versions. These revisions were sometimes done without reference to the original Chinese or Japanese texts, and so they frequently are not literal translations.

Some Western texts are clearer and more inspiring than the original texts from Asia and better suited for the practice of dharma in the new environment. For example, for the "Four (All-Embracing) Vows," I love to chant, "Delusions are inexhaustible. I vow to transform them" (a version by Joan Halifax, chanted at the Upaya Zen Center, Santa Fe), instead of the more common version, "I vow to put an end to them." The former makes much more sense, as we can never "put an end to" delusions or desires.

However, some of the other chants recited nowadays are incomprehensible or even weird, though all of them must have been created with good intention, and people have been chanting them wholeheartedly. For that reason I feel that every chant should be revered as sacred.

All translators, I assume, wish to carry the meanings of the original text as faithfully as possible. But there are differing views as to what "faithful" means. Some may feel that all terms should be accurately translated with the original syntax maintained. Others, including myself, feel that the overall meaning should be transmitted but that, in some cases, deconstruction of the original syntax is unavoidable.

To me, clarity in the translated text is essential. The reader or chanter needs to understand the meaning with as little explanation as possible. Some interpretative phrases may be added if necessary. For example, a word-for-word translation of the first part of the *Ten-Line Life-Affirming Sutra of Avalokiteshvara* would sound something like this: "Avalokiteshvara takes refuge in Buddha, has a cause for a buddha, and has conditions for a buddha." My cotranslator, Joan Halifax, and I added the translation of the name *Avalokiteshvara* in Chinese as "perceiver of the cries of the world." Next, the word *cause* here means "aspiration," so we translated this phrase as "will be a buddha." *Conditions* means "all the supporting elements." Since it is a bodhisattva's vow to bring all beings to the shore of enlightenment before the bodhisattva's own attainment of buddhahood, we translated the last phrase as "helps all to be buddhas." As this example shows, translation is not just the translating of words, but it is also an effort to understand the context, identify the intended meaning in the original text, and reflect the translator's understanding in the translation.

The poetic and literary power of the translated text, as well as its flow of sounds, is also important. What is strong in the original text is not always strong in translation. For example, in the above sutra, the original order of the words describing the quality of Avalokiteshvara is "being eternal, joyful, intimate, and pure." We felt it would be stronger in English if we put *joyful* at the end.

The first line of the *Heart Sutra* in Sanskrit can be translated as "Bodhisattva Avalokiteshvara, moving in the deep course of realizing wisdom beyond wisdom, saw that all five streams of body, heart, and mind are without boundary, and was freed all from anguish." The tense in this text in Sanskrit is past, and the grammatical gender of Avalokiteshvara is masculine. Tense and grammatical gender are rarely used in Chinese. The most recent scholarship indicates that this sutra was created in Chinese first and that the Sanskrit version emerged later.[4] This conjecture justifies our using the Chinese version as the original for our translation and employing the dynamic present tense as follows: "Avalokiteshvara, who helps all to awaken, moves in the deep course of realizing wisdom beyond wisdom, sees that all five streams of body, heart, and mind are without boundary, and frees all from anguish."

The borderline between translation, interpretation, and adaptation is not crystal clear. It varies according to translators and circumstances. The texts of all world religions have histories of reinterpretation and adaptation. In light of the striking differences between various English translations of the Bible, across historical periods and varying cultural positions, we see that our questions about translating Zen texts are not unique. In some cases, for the practice of Zen beyond Asia, sensitively adapted texts make more sense than literal translations. We need to remind ourselves that texts that work in East Asia in their original form may not necessarily address the values of practitioners in the Western world, and vice versa. We should not stubbornly stick to translation; in some cases, we should be open to adaptation.

As mentioned earlier, most East Asian Zen practitioners have kept the same ideographs of the ancient chants and pronounced them in the ways that suited their languages. These chants have been handed down from generation to generation and maintained without change. In such an environment, there is no room for adaptation.

As Zen has spread outside Asia since the mid-twentieth century, different groups have translated these texts into Western languages, often without coordinating with one another. This has made the translations of chants quite diverse. Some groups or teachers went further and adapted the chants more freely to suit their values and needs. This reflects the period we live in, in which a new culture in dharma is rapidly emerging.

Chanting and Singing

Common texts, such as the *Heart Sutra* and the "Four All-Embracing Vows," are recited by groups after Zen meditation. Some practitioners in the West may recite these in Chinese, Japanese, Korean, or Vietnamese, while they may also chant them in English or other European languages.

In Antwerp, Belgium, I asked Luc De Winter, the resident Zen teacher of the Ho Sen Dojo, why they chant only in Sino-Japanese. He answered, "Our sangha members speak six languages. If we chant in Flemish or French, it's not fair to people who speak other languages. As Sino-Japanese is no one's language, it suits us best." In this case Sino-Japanese seems to be functioning like Esperanto.

When groups of people meditate together, they may include an officiating priest or layperson who offers incense and bows to the main image on the altar. The chant leader may then deliver a melodic recitation of the title of the text and then the other participants join in to chant together. Sometimes people sound bells, drums, and/or wooden clackers. Some texts may have simple melodies. Generally speaking, traditional Zen chants are recited in a dimly lit room in a fairly monotonous, simple, and deep voice in a somber fashion.

In the Buddhist tradition, music has been an important element. Dharma music is called *shabda vidya* in Sanskrit, *shengming* in Chinese, and *shomyo* in Japanese. Such dharma music—singing with instrumental accompaniment—is practiced widely in Vajrayana Buddhism, but to a lesser degree in Zen schools. Dogen talks about an event of melodic sutra chanting in his essay "Practice Period."[5] In some Zen centers in the Western world, a melodic chanting of Buddhas' names is practiced in an atonement or vow-renewing ceremony on a full-moon evening.

Zen chants can also be colorful, complex, and joyful. I am aware that at Shasta Abby in California, founded by Jiyu Kennett Roshi, Zen chants are sung in the style of Gregorian chant. Thich Nhat Hanh, a renowned Vietnamese Buddhist teacher, and his community have developed a number of songs for ceremonies and daily practice. One of his many books, *Chanting from the Heart,* lists over forty songs with music scores. They include "Evening Chant," "The Four Reflections," "The Heart of Perfect Understanding (the *Heart Sutra*)," and "Incense Offering." A few of the songs come from traditional Pali or Vietnamese traditions, but all others are contemporary compositions by members of his worldwide community.

I also see an outstanding potential in Luc De Winter's work. He has set some of the chants that Joan Halifax and I translated into English to beautiful choral music. His compositions include the *Ten-Line Sutra of Avalokiteshvara's Boundless Life* (of which a new title is *Ten-Line Life-Affirming Sūtra of Avalokiteshvara*), the *Heart Sutra,* the "Robe Chant," and "Being One and Many," as well as Joan's adaptation of the "Four (All-Embracing) Vows." In 2010, his pieces were sung a cappella by twenty-nine members of the Ensemble Polyfoon in Antwerp. I attended the dress rehearsal and performances of the concert entitled *Sandokai* ("Being One and Many").[6]

The large Cathedral of St. Michael and St. Gudula was packed on both show nights. The intricate weaving of voices by these singers was astoundingly poignant and uplifting. After hearing Buddhist librettos performed in English in a Catholic church, the audience was enthusiastic, offering the musicians cheers and standing ovations.

In December 2011 Joan Halifax invited other Zen teachers to lead an annual intensive retreat at Upaya Zen Center in Santa Fe, New Mexico, to celebrate the Buddha's enlightenment. I was invited as a Buddhist scholar to give dharma talks. Near the end of the last sitting period of the last day, about seventy of us, having sat in silence for seven days, heard the faint voice of a soprano. The singing became louder and clearer, joined by other voices. It was a recording of De Winter's *Ten-Line Sūtra of Avalokiteshvara's Boundless Life*. The composition repeated the verse five times, becoming increasingly complex and ecstatic. Totally surprised, some of the meditators started laughing. Others cried. It was a remarkable and unforgettable experience.

Authenticity in Zen means faithfulness to its heritage. At the same time, we must respect our own cultural and religious backgrounds, and we must remain capable of responding to the needs of the society in which we live. In this respect, I see Luc De Winter's *Sandokai* as having its own form of authenticity. Having been brought up in the Christian tradition and with a love for Renaissance music, Luc naturally incorporated a musical style derived from his own heritage.

I think of myself as an interfaith person—practicing and studying Zen after my childhood exposure to Shinto and Christianity in Japan, and having an affinity for Judaism, Sufism, and Hinduism. This experience inclines me to feel that Zen music and art can incorporate elements of a number of spiritual traditions.

Luc De Winter's choral music has led me to reflect more deeply on cross-cultural streams in Zen during this period of globalization. Have the Asian traditions, while transmitting the wide and profound teachings of Zen, bequeathed their own kinds of narrowness? Should Zen meditation consist mainly of struggles, pain, and self-torture? Can it be comfortable, easy, and joyful? Can practice be open to people of all faiths, ages, races, genders, sexual orientations, and physical conditions and capabilities? Doesn't awakening belong to everyone?

Audio samples of some of the daily chants can be heard at Shambhala.com/zenchants.

Notes to the Reader

Chinese

PINYIN ROMANIZATION is used throughout. In the following list, the right column gives approximate English pronunciations of letters used in the pinyin system (in the left column):

c	ts
q	ch
x	sh
zh	j

For ideographs, the traditional unabridged version is used. Ideographic types are set from left to right.

Japanese

Macrons (to indicate long vowels) are used in the chants and in "The Texts Illuminated" but not in the preface, acknowledgments, or introduction.

Sanskrit

Simplified spellings are used. Macrons and tilde for *ñ* are used only in the chants and in "The Texts Illuminated."

Translation, Adaptation, and Modification Credit

The "Editor" in "The Texts Illuminated" refers to Kazuaki Tanahashi.

Titles of Texts

English titles of books and chapters, followed by their original titles, have been translated by the Editor. Many of these texts exist only in Chinese.

觀世音

南無佛

與佛有因

與佛有緣

佛法僧緣

常樂我淨

朝念觀世音

暮念觀世音

念念從心起

念念不離心

PART ONE

DAILY CHANTS

AWAKENING TOGETHER

All awakened ones
throughout space and time,
honored ones, great beings,
who help all to awaken,
together may we realize
wisdom beyond wisdom!

FOUR ALL-EMBRACING VOWS

Beings are numberless; I vow to awaken them.
Delusions are inexhaustible; I vow to transform them.
Dharmas are boundless; I vow to comprehend them.
The awakened way is incomparable; I vow to embody it.

TEN-LINE LIFE-AFFIRMING SŪTRA OF AVALOKITESHVARA

Avalokiteshvara, perceiver of the cries of the world,
takes refuge in Buddha,
will be a buddha,
helps all to be buddhas,
is not separate from Buddha, Dharma, Sangha—
being eternal, intimate, pure, and joyful.
In the morning, be one with Avalokiteshvara.
In the evening, be one with Avalokiteshvara,
whose heart, moment by moment, arises,
whose heart, moment by moment, remains!

SŪTRA ON THE HEART OF REALIZING WISDOM BEYOND WISDOM

Avalokiteshvara, who helps all to awaken,
moves in the deep course of
realizing wisdom beyond wisdom,
sees that all five streams of
body, heart, and mind are without boundary,
and frees all from anguish.

O Shariputra,
[who listens to the teachings of the Buddha],
form is not separate from boundlessness;
boundlessness is not separate from form.
Form is boundlessness; boundlessness is form.
The same is true of feelings, perceptions, inclinations,
    and discernment.

O Shariputra,
boundlessness is the nature of all things.
Boundlessness neither arises nor perishes,
neither stains nor purifies,
neither increases nor decreases.
Boundlessness is not limited by form,
nor by feelings, perceptions, inclinations, or discernment.
It is free of the eyes, ears, nose, tongue, body, and mind;
free of sight, sound, smell, taste, touch, and any object of mind;
free of sensory realms, including the realm of the mind.

It is free of ignorance and the end of ignorance.
Boundlessness is free of old age and death,
and free of the end of old age and death.
It is free of suffering, arising, cessation, and path,
and free of wisdom and attainment.

Being free of attainment, those who help all to awaken
abide in the realization of wisdom beyond wisdom
and live with an unhindered mind.
Without hindrance, the mind has no fear.
Free from confusion, those who lead all to liberation
embody profound serenity.
All those in the past, present, and future,
who realize wisdom beyond wisdom,
manifest unsurpassable and thorough awakening.

Know that realizing wisdom beyond wisdom
is no other than this wondrous mantra,
luminous, unequaled, and supreme.
It relieves all suffering.
It is genuine and not illusory.

So set forth this mantra of realizing wisdom beyond wisdom.
Set forth this mantra that says:

Gaté, gaté, paragaté, parasamgaté, bodhi! Svahā!

MEAL CHANT

We reflect on the effort that brought us this food and consider
how it comes to us.

We reflect on our practice and service, and whether we are worthy
of this offering.

We regard it as essential to keep the mind free from excess and
greed.

We regard this food as good medicine to sustain our life.

For the sake of awakening, we now receive this food.

ROBE VERSE

Vast is the robe of liberation,
a formless field of benefaction!
I wear the Tathāgata's teaching
to awaken countless beings.

THREE REFUGES

Buddham saranam gacchāmi
Dhammam saranam gacchāmi
Sangham saranam gacchāmi

Dutiyam-pi, Buddham saranam gacchāmi
Dutiyam-pi, dhammam saranam gacchāmi
Dutiyam-pi, sangham saranam gacchāmi

Tatiyam-pi, Buddham saranam gacchāmi
Tatiyam-pi, dhammam saranam gacchāmi
Tatiyam-pi, sangham saranam gacchāmi

METTĀ

Ahaṁ sukhito homi.
Niddukkho homi.
Avero homi.
Abyāpajjho homi.
Anīgho homi.
Sukhī attānam pariharāmi.

Sabbe sattā sukhitā hontu.
Sabbe sattā averā hontu.
Sabbe sattā abyāpajjhā hontu.
Sabbe sattā anīghā hontu.
Sabbe sattā sukhī attānam pariharantu.

GREAT COMPASSIONATE HEART DHĀRANĪ

namu kara tan nō tora yā yā namu ori yā boryo ki chi shifu
   ra ya fuji sato bo yā moko
sato bo yā mo kō kya runi kya yā en sa hara ha e shu tan nō
   ton shā namu shiki rīn to i mō
ori yā boryo ki chi shifu rā ri to bō namu no rā kin ji ki rī
   mo ko ho dō sha mi sa bō
o to jō shu ben o shu in sa bo sa tō no mo bo gyā mo ha te cho
   to ji tō en o bo ryo kī ru
gya chī kya ra chī i kiri mo kō fuji sa tō sa bo sa bō mo ra mo
   rā mo ki mo kī ri to in ku ryō ku ryō ke mo to ryō to ryō ho
   ja ya chī mo ko ho ja ya chī to ra to rā chiri nī shifu ra yā sha
   rō sha rō mo mo ha mo rā ho chi rī i ki i kī shi no shi nō ora
   san fura sha rī ha za ha zān fura sha yā ku ryō ku ryō mo ra ku
   ryō ku ryō ki ri sha rō sha rō shi ri shi rī su ryō su ryō fuji yā
   fuji yā fudo yā fudo yā mi chiri yā nora kin jī chiri shuni
   nō hoya mono somo kō shido yā somo kō moko
shido yā somo kō shido yu kī shifu ra yā somo kō nora kin jī
   somo kō mo ra no ra somo kō
shira su omo gya yā somo kō sobo moko shido yā somo kō
   shaki rā oshi do yā somo kō hodo mogya shido yā somo
   kō nora kin jī ha gyara yā somo kō mo horī shin gyara yā
   somo kō namu kara tan nō tora yā yā namu ori yā boryo
   ki chi shifu ra yā somo kō shite dō modorā hodo yā somo kō

WONDROUS AUSPICIOUS DHĀRANĪ
FOR AVERTING CALAMITIES

nomo san manda motonan oha rachī koto shā sono nan tō jī tō
en gyā gyā gyā kī gyā kī un nun shiu rā shiu rā hara shiu rā
hara shiu rā chishu sā chishu sā chishu rī chishu rī sowa jā
sowa jā sen chi gyā shiri ē sōmōkō

DEDICATION

May the merit of our practice pervade without limit,
and may we with all beings together
realize the awakened way!

BUDDHA ANCESTORS

Prajñā Pāramitā, Mother of All Buddhas, Honored One

Vipashin Buddha, Honored One
Shikhin Buddha, Honored One
Vishvabhū Buddha, Honored One
Krakucchanda Buddha, Honored One
Kanakamuni Buddha, Honored One
Kāshyapa Buddha, Honored One
Shākyamuni Buddha, Honored One

Mahākāshyapa, Honored One
Ānanda, Honored One
Shanavāsin, Honored One
Upagupta, Honored One
Dhritaka, Honored One
Micchaka, Honored One
Vasumitra, Honored One
Buddhanandi, Honored One
Buddhamitra, Honored One
Pārshva, Honored One
Punyayashas, Honored One
Ashvaghosha, Honored One
Kapimala, Honored One
Nāgārjuna, Honored One
Kānadeva, Honored One
Rāhulata, Honored One
Sanghānandi, Honored One

Gayashāta, Honored One
Kumārata, Honored One
Jayata, Honored One
Vasubandhu, Honored One
Manorhita, Honored One
Haklenayashas, Honored One
Simhabhikshu, Honored One
Basiasita, Honored One
Punyamitra, Honored One
Prajñātāra, Honored One

Bodhidharma, Honored One
Dazu Huike, Honored One
Jianzhi Sengcan, Honored One
Dayi Daoxin, Honored One
Daman Hongren, Honored One
Dajian Huineng, Honored One

Nanyue Huairang, Honored One
Mazu Daoyi, Honored One
Baizhang Huaihai, Honored One
Huangbo Xiyun, Honored One
Linji Yixuan, Honored One
Xinghua Cunjiang, Honored One
Nanyuan Huiyong, Honored One
Fengxue Yanzhao, Honored One
Shoushan Xingnian, Honored One
Fenyang Shanzhao, Honored One
Ciming Chuyuan, Honored One
Yangqi Fanghui, Honored One

Qingyuan Xingsi, Honored One
Shitou Xiqian, Honored One
Yaoshan Weiyan, Honored One
Yunyan Tansheng, Honored One
Dongshan Liangjie, Honored One
Yunju Daoying, Honored One
Tongan Daopi, Honored One
Tongan Guanzhi, Honored One
Liangshan Yuanguan, Honored One
Dayang Jingxuan, Honored One
Touzi Yiqing, Honored One
Furong Daokai, Honored One

Haihui Shouduan, Honored One
Wuzu Fayan, Honored One
Yuanwu Keqin, Honored One
Huqiu Shaolong, Honored One
Ying'an Tanhua, Honored One
Mi'an Xianjie, Honored One
Songyuan Chongyue, Honored One
Yun'an Puyan, Honored One
Xutang Zhiyu, Honored One

Nampo Shōmyō, Honored One

Danxia Zichun, Honored One
Changlu Qingliao, Honored One
Tiantong Zongjue, Honored One
Xuedou Zhijian, Honored One
Tiantong Rujing, Honored One

Eihei Dōgen, Honored One
Koun Ejō, Honored One
Tettsū Gikai, Honored One
Keizan Jōkin, Honored One

FEMALE BUDDHA ANCESTORS

Prajñā Pāramitā, Mother of All Buddhas, Honored One

Mahā Māyā, Honored One
Shrīmālā, Honored One
Tārā, Honored One
Ratnavatī, Honored One
Prabhūtā, Honored One
Sinhavijurmbhitā, Honored One

Mahāpajcpati Gotami, Honored One
Khemā, Honored One
Sundarīnandā, Honored One
Patāchārā, Honored One
Bhaddākundalakesā, Honored One
Sumanā, Honored One
Kisāgotamī, Honored One
Dhammā, Honored One
Uppalavannā, Honored One
Yashodharā, Honored One
Somā, Honored One
Sakulā, Honored One
Bhaddākapilānī, Honored One
Singālakapitā, Honored One
Sāmāvatī, Honored One
Sanghamittā Theri , Honored One
Prasannasillā, Honored One

Jingjian, Honored One
Zongji, Honored One
Lingzhao, Honored One
Ling Xingpo, Honored One
Moshan Liaoran, Honored One
Liu Tiemo, Honored One
Miaoxin, Honored One
Shiji, Honored One
Juhan Daojen, Honored One
Daoshen, Honored One
Huiguang, Honored One
Huiwen, Honored One
Fadeng, Honored One
Yu Daopo, Honored One
Miaodao, Honored One
Zhidong, Honored One
Miaozong, Honored One
Qinguo, Honored One
Miaohui, Honored One
Zhiyuan Xinggang, Honored One
Jizong Xingche, Honored One
Jifu Zukui, Honored One
Shenyi, Honored One

Zenshin, Honored One
Kōmyō, Honored One
Ryōnen, Honored One
Shōgaku, Honored One
Egi, Honored One
Mugai Nyodai, Honored One
Kakuzan Shidō, Honored One
Ekan, Honored One

Kontō Ekyū, Honored One
Mokufū, Honored One
Sōitsu, Honored One
Eshun, Honored Onc
Yōdō, Honored One
Kōgetsu, Honored One
Sōshin, Honored One
Tenshū, Honored One
Daitsū Bunchi, Honored One
Ryōnen Gensō, Honored One
Someko Tachibana, Honored One
Tokugon Rihō, Honored One
Satsu, Honored One
Ōhashi, Honored One
Teijitsu, Honored One
Rengetsu Otagaki, Honored One
Temmyō Jōrin Mizuno, Honored One
Mitsu Hori, Honored One
Sōzen Nagasawa, Honored One
Myōdō Satomi, Honored One
Kendō Kojima, Honored One
Eshun Yoshida, Honored One
Jōshin Kasai, Honored One
Sumiko Kudō, Honored One

Ruth Eryū Jōkei Fuller, Honored One
Maurine Myō-on Stuart, Honored One
Hōun Jiyū Kennett, Honored One
Gesshin Myōkō Prabhasa Dharma Cheney, Honored One
Baihō Trudy Dixon, Honored One

ATONEMENT

For all my unwholesome actions since olden times,
from my beginningless greed, hatred, and ignorance,
born of my body, speech, and thought,
I now fully atone.

REMINDER

Life and death are of grave importance—
impermanent and swift.
Wake up, all of you.
Do not waste your life.

觀世音　南無佛　與佛有因　與佛有緣　佛法僧緣　常樂我淨　朝念觀世音　暮念觀世音　念念從心起　念念不離心

PART TWO

CHANTS FOR EVENTS

OPENING THE SŪTRA VERSE

The unsurpassable, profound, subtle, and wondrous dharma
is rarely met even in a hundred, thousand, myriad eons.
Now we see it, hear it, receive it, and maintain it.
May we realize the Tathāgata's true meaning!

CHANT FOR FORMAL MEALS

VERSE FOR HEARING THE MALLET

Buddha was born in Kapilavastu,
enlightened in Magadha,
taught in Vārānasī,
entered nirvāna in Kushinagara.

CHANT FOR FORMAL MEALS

Setting Out the Bowls

We now set out
utensils of the Tathāgata.
May the three wheels in boundlessness
be equally liberated!

CHANT FOR FORMAL MEALS

INVOCATION

Pure dharmakāya, Vairochana Buddha
Complete sambhogakāya, Rochana Buddha
Numerous nirmānakāya, Shākyamuni Buddhas
Future Maitreya Buddha
All buddhas throughout space and time
Mahāyāna Saddharma Pundarīka Sūtra
Great sacred Mañjushrī Bodhisattva
Mahāyāna Samantabhadra Bodhisattva
Great compassionate Avalokiteshvara Bodhisattva
All honorable bodhisattvas mahāsattvas
Mahā Prajñā Pāramitā

CHANT FOR FORMAL MEALS

OFFERING FOOD FOR SPIRITS

Oh spirits
in the ten directions,
now we offer all of you
this food.

CHANT FOR FORMAL MEALS

Raising the Bowl

The upper part is for the three treasures;
The middle part is for the four benefactors;
The lower part is for all beings in the six paths.
May all be equally nourished!

The first spoonful is to end unwholesome actions.
The second is to cultivate wholesome actions.
The third is to awaken all beings.
Together may we realize the awakened way!

CHANT FOR FORMAL MEALS

Offering Rinse Water

The water with which we wash our bowls
tastes like ambrosia.
We offer it to numberless spirits.
May they be satisfied!
OM MA KU RA SAI SO WA KA.

CHANT FOR FORMAL MEALS

Verse of Pure Practice

Abiding in this world of endless space,
a lotus flower is not stained by muddy water.
We follow the unsurpassable one,
whose mind remains pure and free.

UNIVERSAL PRECEPTS OF THE SEVEN ORIGINAL BUDDHAS

Refrain from unwholesome action.
Engage in wholesome action.
Purify your own mind.
This is the teaching of all buddhas.

MAINTAINING THE PRECEPTS

THE TRUE TEACHING

I take refuge in the Buddha.
I take refuge in the Dharma.
I take refuge in the Sangha.

THE THREE UNIVERSAL PURE PRECEPTS

I vow to observe the precepts.
I vow to take wholesome actions.
I vow to benefit all beings.

THE TEN PROHIBITORY PRECEPTS

I vow not to kill.
I vow not to steal.
I vow not to misuse sex.
I vow not to talk falsely.
I vow not to use intoxicants.
I vow not to speak of the faults of others.
I vow not to praise myself and diminish others.
I vow not to withhold dharma treasures.
I vow not to indulge anger.
I vow not to slander the three treasures.

ADMONITION

Shūhō Myōchō

You who have come to this monastery
and assembled in search of the way,
do not be concerned about your clothing or meals.
As long as you have shoulders, you will have things to wear.
As long as you have a mouth, you will have something to eat.

Just keep exploring what is inconceivable
as you come and go throughout the day.
Time passes swiftly like an arrow.
Value your precious moments,
and do not be caught by trifles.
Be aware! Stay aware!

After I set off on my final journey,
you may want to have a prosperous monastery
with sūtra books and buildings
decorated with gold and silver
attracting a huge, noisy crowd.
Or you may recite sūtras and dhāranīs,
sit for long periods without lying down,
eat one meal only at dawn,
and circumambulate for half of the day.

However hard you would practice in this manner,
if you don't carry in your heart

the wondrous way that is beyond
transmission by buddha ancestors,
you would be nothing but a band of crooked demons,
denying causation and
making the true teaching fall to the ground.
Even a long time after I leave this world,
you would not be allowed to call yourselves
my dharma descendants.

But one of you may live in a field,
in a hut thatched with a single bundle of grass,
and survive on wild herb roots
boiled in a broken-legged pot.
If you devote yourself wholeheartedly
to clarify the single matter,
you will receive my guidance every day
and respond to me in kind.
Who could ignore this?

Endeavor! Endeavor!

念 念 暮 朝 常 佛 與 與 南 觀
念 念 念 念 樂 法 佛 佛 無 世
不 從 觀 觀 我 僧 有 有 佛 音
離 心 世 世 淨 緣 緣 因
心 起 音 音

PART THREE

ENLIGHTENMENT POEMS

ENGRAVING TRUST IN THE HEART
attributed to Jianzhi Sengcan

The utmost way is not difficult.
Just be free of preferences.
Without attachment or aversion,
all becomes transparent.

Missing the way by a hairbreadth,
you separate earth from sky.
If you want to see the way as it is,
do not affirm or deny it.

Dividing things by opposites
is a disease of the mind.
By not seeing the subtle essence,
you lose your serenity.

The circle of the way is boundless space.
There is nothing lacking, nothing extra.
Grasping and discarding
will not bring you there.

Do not pursue external conditions,
nor abide in futile asceticism.
Maintain a peaceful heart,
letting the way be invisible.

Stillness and motion return to stillness.
Stillness turns into motion.
If you are caught in either,
how can you know they are inseparable?

If oneness does not prevail,
the opposites cannot flow freely.
Let existence hide existence.
Pursuing boundlessness betrays boundlessness.

Too many words and thoughts
do not accord with the way.
Free from words and thoughts,
returning to the source,
you go beyond teachings to awakening.

Awakening even for a moment
takes you beyond thoughts on emptiness.
Ideas about emptiness change,
as all of them are illusory.

Pursuing the truth is useless.
Just stop looking.
Do not harbor dualistic views;
refrain from following them.

The slightest idea of right and wrong
fragments the mind.
Two views come from one view;
don't cling to even one view.

When the single mind is not yet born,
the myriad things are undivided:
no separation, no myriad things,
no birth, no mind.

Pursuing the subject, the object vanishes.
Chasing the object, the subject is obscured.
Object is object because of the subject.
Subject is subject because of the object.

How are they related?
Their source is the same boundlessness.
Without boundary, the two are indistinguishable,
each embracing the myriad forms.

Not discriminating between coarse and fine,
how can you be attached to either?
The great way is relaxed,
neither easy nor difficult.

Those with a narrow view are filled with doubt,
going in circles quickly or slowly.
When grasping overtakes you,
you are sure to go astray.

Surrender with ease.
The essence neither leaves nor stays.
If your nature is in accord with the way,
you wander freely without fear.

Caught in thoughts, you betray reality.
Trapped in delusion, you miss the point.
Weary with what is not clear,
what is the use of being near or far?

Do not favor the single path
or disfavor the six-sense objects.
The objects of our senses are not unwholesome.
They are inseparable from authentic awakening.

The wise do not make things happen.
Fools are caught by doing.
Things are no more than things.
Don't be deceived by attachments.

To reveal the mind with the mind—
is it not a great mistake?
Delusion divides stillness from turmoil.
Enlightenment does not pick and choose.

All things have two sides.
Mistakenly, you waver between this and that.
Dreams, phantoms, blossoms of illusion—
why try to grasp them?

Gain and loss, right and wrong—
let go of them right now.
When your eyes are not shut,
then all dreaming ceases.

If your mind makes no distinctions,
all things are as they are.

Thusness is subtle,
being free from all conditions.

Seeing all things as equal,
you return to suchness.
Bring to an end all causes,
and let go of all comparisons.

Motion in stillness is not motion.
Stillness in motion is not stillness.
When neither happens,
neither is there.

In the ultimate freedom,
there are no doctrines.
When your mind merges with impartiality,
both making and being made disappear.

While doubts exhaust the pure heart,
genuine trust is plain and simple.
In it nothing remains,
and nothing is remembered.

Space illuminates itself,
not requiring mental effort.
In the realm beyond thinking,
thoughts and feelings are not measured.

In the dharma world of true thusness,
there is no self, no other.
To explain it briefly:
just say, "Not two."

Nonduality has no distinctions.
It leaves out nothing.
The wise in the ten directions
abide in the original source.

This source is timeless.
One moment is ten thousand years.
Time exists and does not exist.
The ten directions are right here.

The extremely small is vast;
it leaps beyond boundaries.
The extremely large is minute;
you cannot define it.

Existence is itself nonexistence.
Nonexistence is itself existence.
If reality is not like this,
it will never continue.

One is inseparable from all.
All is inseparable from one.
If you realize this,
you go beyond thinking.

Trust in the heart is not-two.
Not-two is trust in the heart.
Words, unspoken,
go beyond past, present, and future.

SONG OF REALIZING THE WAY
Yongjia Xuanjiao

1
Don't you see?

A person beyond study, not-doing in the leisurely way,
neither removes delusion nor searches for truth.
The true nature of ignorance is itself buddha nature.
This empty, transient, phantom body is itself the dharma body.

Once realized,
there is not a single thing.
The original source of self nature is a true buddha.
The floating clouds of five streams come and go in emptiness.
The bubbles of three poisons appear and vanish in the void.

When reality is grasped,
there are no humans or dharmas—
immediately the karma of falling into Avīchi Hell disappears.
But if you deceive sentient beings with false words,
your tongue will be cut out for countless eons.

If you suddenly realize the Tathāgata's Zen,
all activities of the six realizations will fill your body.
In a dream there are six paths bright and clear;
after awakening, throughout emptiness,
the billion worlds do not exist.

Neither fault nor fortune, loss nor gain—
within nirvāna there is nothing to look for.
Until now, the stained mirror has not been polished.
Today you should discern it clearly.

Who is beyond thought, beyond birth?
Truly beyond birth is beyond no-birth.
Call out and ask a wooden puppet
how soon you will receive merit by trying to become a buddha.

2
Let go of the four great elements without grasping—
just eat and drink in serenity.
All phenomena are impermanent and empty.
This is the complete realization of the Tathāgata.

A true monk expresses a genuine teaching,
and, with passion, persuades those who doubt.
For cutting the root of delusion—a mark of the Buddha—
there is no time to pick leaves and look for branches.

People do not recognize the wish-granting jewel,
although they receive it in the Tathāgata's treasury.
When the six miraculous powers work, emptiness is beyond
    emptiness.
In the circular light of a pearl, form is beyond form.

Even five eyes that are pure
with five excellent powers
cannot fathom the insight of realization.

To see forms in the mirror is not difficult,
but how can you grasp the moon in water?

One who journeys alone always walks alone.
All masters travel leisurely in the path of nirvāna.
If you harmonize with the ancient, your spirit will be high,
although people may shun you as weary and gaunt.

3
Starving monks praise poverty,
but they are not lacking in their practice of the way.
Though poor and wearing tatters,
when you practice the way, there is a priceless treasure
    in your heart.

What is priceless is used without limit.
When needed, benefiting others is never withheld.
Three bodies and four wisdoms are complete in your body.
Eight liberations and six miraculous powers are marked
    in your mind.

People with full capacity hear once and understand completely.
Those with ordinary capacity hear much but still distrust.
If you open your stained robe and see within,
why would you boast of your effort?

Let others slander and criticize.
Trying to grab fire and burn heaven is exhausting.
To hear the Buddha's words is like drinking nectar
that melts doubt and lets you merge with the inconceivable.

There is benefit to observing hateful speech;
it makes you a good guiding teacher.
If you don't hold a grudge against those who slander,
you don't need to express patience and compassion.

The source penetrates and so do words.
Samādhi and wisdom are clear when not stuck in emptiness.
You do not realize it alone, but
with as many buddhas as the sands of the Ganges.

The lion's roar expounds fearlessness,
while all listening animals crush their brains.
A fragrant elephant splashes water, losing its dignity.
A heavenly dragon quietly listens and arouses joy.

4
Wandering on lakes and seas, crossing mountains and rivers,
you look for teachers and practice Zen, inquiring of the way.
When you attain Caoxi's path,
you understand that birth and death are not in opposition.

Walking is Zen; sitting is Zen.
In speaking, silence, movement, and stillness, your body
    is at ease.
Threatened by spears or swords, you do not lose composure.
Even if you are poisoned, you are not disturbed.

Our master Shākyamuni saw Dīpankara Buddha eons ago
and became the Sorcerer of Patience.

After many rounds of birth and death,
he realized that the cycle continues without ceasing.

Then he suddenly saw what is beyond birth,
where nothing is either joyous or worrisome in glory
    or shame.
He entered the mountains and lived in retreat
    under a tall pine tree on a steep cliff.
Serenely, he sat in a monk's outdoor abode.
His peaceful dwelling was indeed solitary and plain.

5
Awakening is complete by itself, free of the merit of giving.
All endeavors have various effects.
Being generous in order to be born in the deva world
is just like shooting an arrow into the air.

When the force is lost, the arrow drops.
Trying to obtain a good future birth won't work,
unlike the gate of reality beyond endeavor,
where you enter the Tathāgata realm with a single leap.

Just realize the essence, unconcerned with the rest.
It's like the moon in pure lapis lazuli.
If you understand this wish-granting jewel,
benefiting self and others never ends.

The river moon shines while pine winds blow.
What happens on a clear winter evening?

The precept jewel of buddha nature is in the mind realm.
Mist, dew, cloud, and haze are its outer robe.

Whether subduing a dragon with a bowl or pacifying
    tigers with a staff,
the golden rings on the two-prong thunderbolt resound.
Instead of being useless,
these tools manifest the Tathāgata's walking stick.

6
I neither seek truth nor try to cut delusion,
since I know that both are empty and formless.
No form, no emptiness, no beyond-emptiness:
this is the Tathāgata's reality.

The mind mirror is clear without hindrance,
broadly reflecting the infinite world.
Myriad forms and all phenomena appear;
the circular light of a pearl has no inside or outside.

An absolute view of emptiness that ignores cause and effect
endlessly invites calamity.
Abandoning existence and being attached to emptiness is also this
    sickness.
It is like jumping into fire to avoid drowning.

Let go of your deluded mind and grasp truth.
A mind that picks and chooses creates clever deception.
Without understanding this, students rely on it in practice.
Through seeing deeply, the thief is recognized as one's child.

We harm the dharma treasure and diminish merit
by always depending on this deception.
Thus, in the Zen gate, we clarify this mind
and quickly realize beyond-birth.

7
A courageous person takes up a wisdom sword.
A spear of prajñā is indeed a vajra flame.
They not only crush the mind of those outside the way,
but swiftly gouge out a demon's guts.

Dharma thunder beats the drum,
spreading clouds of compassion that rain down nectar.
Dragons and elephants continuously stomp the wetland,
awakening the Three Vehicles and five capacities.

Pure milk from the Snow Mountains
turns into nourishing cream.
Dharma nature is complete, as are all natures.
One dharma includes all dharmas.

One moon appears in waters everywhere.
The moon in all waters is one inclusive moon.
The dharma body of all buddhas enters our nature.
Our nature merges with the Tathāgata.

One land embodies all lands.
Not form, not mind, not action,
a finger snap completes eighty thousand gates.
A moment destroys the karma of countless eons.

No verses are verses.
What will you do with spiritual awakening?
Do not slander or praise.
The essence is vast and open, with neither cliff nor shore.

It is abundant right where you are.
In seeking it, just know you cannot see.
You cannot grasp or let go of it.
Just realize thusness in what you cannot grasp.

Speak while being silent and be silent while you speak.
The great gate of giving opens with no obstruction.
If someone asks the source of my teaching,
I say: "The power of great prajñā."

You may not understand when I speak of this or not-this;
even heaven may not follow when I go back and forth.
But in the past I studied scriptures for eons,
so don't think I mean to groundlessly confuse.

8
The essentials of establishing dharma and raising the banner
are clear in the Buddha's words and Caoxi's sayings.
First, Mahākāshyapa received the lamp,
and twenty-eight generations in India confirmed it.

Then the dharma flowed through rivers and oceans to China,
where Bodhidharma became the First Ancestor.
Transmission of the robe in the first six generations is well known.
Numberless people in later generations attained the way.

Truth is not established; illusion is originally void.
With no affirmation or negation, emptiness is not emptiness.
Do not cling to the twenty gates of emptiness.
One Tathāgata nature covers all.

Mind reflects senses; phenomena are dust.
Both of them blur the mirror.
Only when the mirror is cleaned can light emerge.
When both mind and phenomena drop away, the essence is clear.

Ah, this unwholesome time of declining dharma!
Sentient beings are thin on happiness and hard to guide.
With the ancient sages gone, crooked views grow deep;
demons are strong, dharma is weak, and disasters spread.

How regrettable that people don't enter the Tathāgata's gate
of sudden enlightenment and shatter their delusions like tiles.
Intention resides in the mind; disaster is in the body.
It makes no sense to be sorry and blame others.

9
If you do not want to incur the karma of Avīchi Hell,
do not slander the Tathāgata's authentic dharma wheel.
No ordinary plants grow beside the sandalwood tree.
Deep in the serene forest, a lion abides.

When a lion walks alone,
other animals flee and birds fly away.
A lion cub is followed by many attendants.
After three years it makes a great roar.

When a wild fox accompanies the dharma king,
even a ghost that haunted it for one hundred years becomes still.

The complete immediate teaching is beyond human thought.
Let those who are uncertain debate.
I am not insisting on my own view
but warning of the pits of permanence and annihilation.

Denying and not denying, affirming and not affirming—
the slightest discrepancy makes you miss by one thousand miles.
Affirmed, a dragon princess immediately attained buddhahood;
denied, the monk Sunakshatra went straight to hell.

When young, I studied hard,
examining commentaries, reading sūtras and treatises,
analyzing names and meanings, without yet understanding.
I grew exhausted in the ocean sands of letters.

I was admonished by the Tathāgata:
What was the use of counting others' treasure?
I realized that by wandering about for many years
I had lost the way.

10
Those with an unfortunate upbringing and mistaken views
miss the complete immediate teaching of the Tathāgata.
Endeavor in the Two Vehicles is not the heart of the way;
the cleverness of those outside the way is not wisdom.

How foolish and ignorant!

A fist or finger may be misunderstood as true understanding.
Working hard to see the finger as the moon
creates confusion in matters of subject and object.

Beyond seeing even one thing is the Tathāgata,
who is called the One Who Sees Freely.
Know that the hindrance of karma is originally empty.
Before realization, you keep paying off your debt.

You are invited to a royal feast but cannot eat;
you meet the Medicine King but cannot be healed.
But, in the midst of delusion, if you practice Zen and pursue
    insight,
the lotus will grow in fire without perishing.

Even the monk Suradatta, who committed grave offenses,
    realized beyond-birth,
quickly became a buddha, and remains one now.
A lion's roar expounds the teaching of no fear.
I lament the stubborn ignorance of those who don't
    understand.

They only know that committing crimes hinders enlightenment
but do not see that the Tathāgata reveals the secret.
There were two monks who committed murder and rape.
The monk Upāli's trivial advice only made their crimes worse.

Vimalakīrti immediately removed their doubt,
like a bright sun that melts frost and snow.
Wondrous is the power of liberation
that works endlessly.

11

The four types of offering are not spared;
myriad pieces of gold can be spent.
Grinding bones and crushing flesh is not enough;
clarifying one phrase goes beyond a billion words.

The king of dharma is unsurpassable,
tathāgatas as many as the sands of the Ganges realize together.
I now elucidate this wish-granting jewel;
may all who receive it be blessed!

When you see through, there is not one thing—
no person, no buddha.
A billion worlds are bubbles in the ocean;
all sages disappear like lightning.

Even if a red-hot disk rotates on your head,
samādhi's bright and complete wisdom will not be lost.
Were the sun cold and the moon hot,
demons could not destroy the true teaching.

When an elephant carriage roars slowly forward,
who could imagine a praying mantis blocking its way?
A great elephant does not wander a hare's path;
great enlightenment is not concerned with minor knots.

Do not slander the vast blue sky with limited views.
If you don't yet have it, this is for you.

BEING ONE AND MANY
Shitou Xiqian

The heart of the great sage of India
is intimately transmitted east and west.

Humans can be wise and foolish,
but the way has no northern or southern ancestors.

The source is clear and bright.
Branching streams flow in the dark.

Being attached to things is delusion.
Understanding reality is not yet enlightenment.

Senses and their fields intermingle
yet are distinct.

When they interact,
they go beyond their conditions.

Each thing has its unique quality.
Sounds can be shrill or joyful.

In darkness, all words are one.
In brightness, phrases are murky or clear.

The four elements return to their source,
like a child to its mother.

Fire is hot; wind moves.
Water is wet; earth is solid.

The eye sees color; the ear hears sound;
the nose smells; the tongue tastes salty or sour.

The root of each thing
causes branches and leaves to flourish.

Trunk and twig share the essence.
Words distinguish one from the other.

Within brightness, there is darkness,
but do not seek the darkness.

Within darkness, there is brightness,
but do not look for the brightness.

Brightness and darkness contrast with each other,
like the front and back foot in walking.

Each thing has its own virtue,
And is named according to place and function.

Things fit together, as a box and its lid.
Merging with reality, arrow points meet in midair.

Understand the true meaning of words.
Do not set up your own standards.

If the way does not meet your eyes,
will your feet know the path?

Going forward is beyond far and near.
When you are lost, mountains and rivers are unreachable.

Let me respectfully remind you who engage in deep practice:
time passes swiftly; do not squander your life.

SONG OF THE GRASS HUT

Shitou Xiqian

I've built a grass hut where there's nothing of value.
After eating, I relax and enjoy a nap.

When it was completed, fresh weeds appeared.
Now it's been lived in—covered by weeds.

The person in the hut lives here calmly,
not stuck to inside, outside, or in-between.

Places worldly people live, I don't live.
Realms worldly people love, I don't love.

Though the hut is small, it includes the entire world.
In ten feet square, an old man illumines forms and their nature.

A Mahāyāna bodhisattva trusts without doubt.
The middling or lowly can't help wondering:

Will this hut perish or not?
Perishable or not, the original master is present.

The experience of not dwelling south or north, east or west,
firmly based in steadiness—it can't be surpassed.

A shining window below the green pines—
jade palaces or vermilion towers can't compare with it.

Just sitting with head covered, all things are at rest.
Thus, this mountain monk doesn't understand at all.

Living here he no longer works to get free.
Who would proudly arrange seats, trying to entice guests?

Turn the light around to shine within; then just return.
The vast inconceivable source can't be faced or turned away from.

Meet the ancestral teachers, be familiar with their instructions,
bind grasses to build a hut, and don't give up.

Let go of hundreds of years and relax completely.
Open your hands and walk, innocent.

Thousands of words, myriad interpretations,
are only to free you from obstructions.

If you want to know the undying person in the hut,
don't separate from this skin bag here and now.

THE JEWEL MIRROR AWARENESS
Dongshan Liangjie

The dharma of thusness
is intimately conveyed by buddha ancestors.

Now you have it;
keep it well.

A silver bowl filled with snow,
a heron hiding in moonlight—

they are similar but not the same.
Side by side, you can see the difference.

The meaning is not in the words,
yet one pivotal instant can reveal it.

Move and you are trapped;
miss it, and you fall into confusion and doubt.

Turning away and touching are both wrong,
for it is like a massive fire.

To depict it with complex words
is to defile it.

In the darkest night,
dawn is not revealed.

It acts as a guide for beings.
Its use removes all suffering.

Although it is not created,
it is not beyond words.

It is like facing a jeweled mirror;
form and image behold each other.

You are not it;
yet it is you.

Like a newborn child,
who is endowed with five aspects,

no coming, no going,
no arising, no abiding.

"Baba wawa"—
is there anything said or not?

In truth, this has no meaning,
for the words are not yet clear.

Like the horizontal lines of the double "fire" hexagram,
the dual and nondual integrate.

Folded up, they make three;
the complete transformation makes five.

It is like the taste of a five-flavored herb
or like the diamond thunderbolt.

Wondrously within nonduality,
drumming and singing go together.

Penetrating the source and traveling the way,
you go through a narrow path.

Complications are auspicious;
do not resist them.

What is natural and inconceivable,
belongs neither to delusion nor enlightenment.

Causes and conditions at this moment
shine completely in the silence.

So fine, it enters nowhere;
so vast, it exceeds all bounds.

A hairbreadth deviation,
and you are out of harmony.

Through the teachings of sudden and gradual,
different methods have arisen.

Even though you master such teachings,
the truth keeps on escaping.

Sitting still, yet inwardly moving,
is like a tethered colt, a trapped rat.

The ancestors pitied them
and offered them the teachings.

According to your delusions,
black is white.

When delusions disappear,
the natural mind reveals itself.

If you want to follow the ancient path,
please observe teachers of former times.

Some try to attain the buddha way
by gazing at a tree for ten eons.

They are like a tiger with tattered ears
or a hobbled horse.

With low aspirations,
you seek jeweled pedestals and fine clothing.

With a sense of wonder,
you make a black badger a white bull.

Yi, with his archer's skill,
could hit the mark from a hundred paces.

When arrow points meet head on,
how could it be a matter of skill?

The wooden man begins to sing,
and the stone woman gets up to dance.

This does not come by knowing,
nor does it involve ideas.

Ministers serve their lords;
children obey their guardians.

Not obeying is not filial;
failure to serve is of no help.

Practice invisibly, work intimately,
be the fool with no voice.

One who can continue this
is called a "host within the host."

THE POINT OF ZAZEN
Eihei Dōgen

The hub of buddhas' activity,
the turning of the ancestors' hub,
moves along beyond thinking
and is completed in the realm of beyond merging.

As it moves along beyond thinking,
its appearing is immediate.
As it is completed in the realm of beyond merging,
completeness itself is realization.

When its appearing is intimate,
you have no illusion.
When completeness reveals itself,
it is neither real nor apparent.

When you have immediacy without illusion,
immediacy is "dropping away" with no obstacles.
Realization, beyond real or apparent,
is effort without expectation.

Clear water all the way to the bottom:
a fish swims like a fish.
Vast sky transparent throughout:
a bird flies like a bird.

IN PRAISE OF ZAZEN
Hakuin Ekaku

Sentient beings are in essence buddhas.
It is like water and ice.

There is no ice without water;
there are no buddhas outside of sentient beings.

What a shame, sentient beings seek afar,
not knowing what is at hand.

It is like wailing from thirst
in the midst of water

or wandering lost among the poor,
although born a rich family's child.

The cause of rebirth in the six realms
is the darkness of our delusion.

Treading one dark path after another,
when can we escape birth and death?

Mahāyāna Zen meditation
goes beyond all praise.

Giving, keeping precepts, and the other realizations,
chanting Buddha's name, repentance, training, and

many other kinds of wholesome deeds
all find their source in zazen.

When you sit even once,
the merit obliterates countless wrongdoings.

How can there be unwholesome realms?
The Pure Land is not far.

If, by good fortune, you have the occasion
to hear this teaching,

admire it, and rejoice in it,
you will attain limitless happiness.

How much more if you dedicate yourself
and realize your own nature directly.

This own-nature is no nature.
You are already apart from useless discussions.

The gate opens where cause and effect are inseparable.
The road of not-two, not-three goes straight ahead.

Make the form formless form,
going and returning, not anywhere else.

Make the thought thoughtless thought,
singing and dancing, the dharma voice.

How vast the sky of unobstructed concentration!
How brilliant the full moon of four wisdoms!

At this very moment, what can be sought?
Nirvāna is immediate.

This place is the lotus land.
This body is the buddha body.

觀世音 南無佛 與佛有因 與佛有緣 佛法僧緣 常樂我淨 朝念觀世音 暮念觀世音 念念從心起 念念不離心

PART FOUR

PROSE CHANTS FOR STUDY

RECOMMENDING ZAZEN TO ALL PEOPLE
Eihei Dōgen

THE REAL WAY circulates everywhere; how could it require practice or enlightenment? The essential teaching is fully available; how could effort be necessary? Furthermore, the entire mirror is free of dust; why take steps to polish it? Nothing is separate from this very place; why journey away?

And yet, if you miss the mark even by a strand of hair, you are as distant as heaven from earth. If the slightest discrimination occurs, you will be lost in confusion. You could be proud of your understanding and have abundant realization, or acquire outstanding wisdom and attain the way by clarifying the mind. Still, if you are wandering about in your head, you may miss the vital path of letting your body leap.

You should observe the example of the Buddha Shākyamuni of the Jeta Grove, who practiced sitting up straight for six years even though he was gifted with intrinsic wisdom. Still celebrated is Master Bodhidharma of Shaolin Temple, who sat facing the wall for nine years, although he had already received the mind seal. Ancient sages were like this; who nowadays does not need to practice as they did?

Hence, you should stop searching for phrases and chasing after words. Take the backward step and turn the light inward. Your body-mind of itself will drop off, and your original face will appear. If you want to attain just this, immediately practice just this.

For zazen, a quiet room is appropriate. Drink and eat in moderation. Let go of all involvements and let myriad things rest. Do not think good or bad. Do not judge right or wrong. Stop conscious endeavor and analytic introspection. Do not try to become a buddha. How could being a buddha be limited to sitting or not sitting? In an appropriate place for sitting, set out a thick mat and put a round cushion on top of it. Sit either in the full- or half-lotus posture. For the full-lotus posture, first place the right foot on the left thigh, then the left foot on the right thigh. For the half-lotus posture, place the left foot on the right thigh. Loosen the robes and belts, and arrange them in an orderly way. Then place the right hand palm up on the left foot, and the left hand on the right hand, lightly touching the ends of the thumbs together. Sit straight up without leaning to the right or left and without bending forward or backward. The ears should be in line with the shoulders and the nose in line with the navel. Rest the tongue against the roof of the mouth, with lips and teeth closed. Keep the eyes open, and breathe gently through the nose.

Having adjusted your body in this manner, take a breath and exhale fully; then sway your body to left and right. Now sit steadfastly and think not-thinking. How do you think not-thinking? Beyond thinking. This is the essential art of zazen.

The zazen I speak of is not learning meditation. It is simply the dharma gate of enjoyment and ease. It is the practice-realization of complete enlightenment. Realize the fundamental point, free from the binding of nets and baskets. Once you experience it, you are like a dragon swimming in the water or a tiger reposing in the mountains. Know that the true dharma emerges of itself, clearing away hindrances and distractions.

When you stand up from sitting, move your body slowly and rise calmly, without haste. We understand from past precedents that going beyond ordinary and sacred, where sitting and standing are effortless and boundless, depends solely on the power of zazen.

Furthermore, bringing forth the turning point by using a finger, a pole, a needle, or a mallet, or leading people to enlightenment with a whisk, a fist, a stick, or a shout cannot be understood by discriminatory thinking. How can it be understood by the use of supernatural powers? Zazen is an awesome presence outside form and color. How is it not the path preceding concept?

Thus, do not be concerned with who is wise and who is stupid. Do not discriminate the sharp from the dull. To practice wholeheartedly is the true endeavor of the way. Practice-realization is not defiled with specialness; it is a matter for every day.

Now, in this world and in other worlds, in India and China, buddha ancestors equally carry the buddha seal and teach to sit immersed in steadfastness. Although circumstances may vary in a thousand ways, wholeheartedly practice Zen, giving yourself fully to the way. Why give up the sitting platform of your own house and wander uselessly in the dust of a remote land? Once a wrong step is taken, you depart from the way.

Having received a human life, do not waste the passing moments. Already upholding the buddha way, why would you indulge in the sparks from a flint? After all, form is like a dewdrop on the grass. Human life is like a flash of lightning, transient and illusory, gone in a moment.

Honored practitioners of Zen, please do not grope for the elephant or try to grasp the true dragon. Strive to hit the mark by directly pointing. Revere the mind that goes beyond study and surpasses all doings. Experience the enlightenment of the buddhas, correctly inheriting the samādhi of the ancestors. Practice thusness continuously, and you will be thus. The treasury will open of itself for you to use as you wish.

ON THE ENDEAVOR OF THE WAY
Eihei Dōgen

ALL BUDDHA TATHĀGATAS who individually transmit inconceivable dharma, actualizing unsurpassable, complete enlightenment, have a wondrous art, supreme and unconditioned. Receptive
samādhi is its mark; only buddhas transmit it to buddhas without
veering off. Sitting upright, practicing Zen, is the authentic gate to
free yourself in the unconfined realm of this samādhi.

Although this inconceivable dharma is abundant in each person, it is not actualized without practice, and it is not experienced
without realization. When you release it, it fills your hand—how
could it be limited to one or many? When you speak it, it fills your
mouth—it is not bounded by length or width.

All buddhas continuously abide in this dharma and do not leave
traces of consciousness about where they are. Sentient beings continuously move about in this dharma, but where they are is not
clear in their consciousness.

The concentrated endeavor of the way I am speaking of allows
all things to come forth in realization to practice going beyond in
the path of letting go. Passing through the barrier [of dualism] and
dropping off limitations in this way, how could you be hindered by
nodes in bamboo or knots in wood [concepts and theories]?

After the aspiration for enlightenment arose, I began to search
for dharma, visiting teachers at various places in our country. Then
I met the priest Myōzen, of the Kennin Monastery, with whom I
trained for nine years, and thus I learned a little about the teaching
of the Rinzai School. The priest Myōzen alone, as a senior disciple of the ancestor Eisai, authentically received transmission of the

unsurpassable buddha dharma from him; no one can be compared with the priest Myōzen.

Later I went to great Song China, visited masters on both sides of the Zhe River, and heard the teachings of the Five Gates. Finally, I became a student of the Zen master Rujing, of Taibo Peak, and completed my life's quest of the great matter.

Then, at the beginning of Shaoding era [1228–1233 C.E.] of great Song, I came back to Japan with the vision of spreading the teaching and saving sentient beings—a heavy burden on my shoulders. And yet I have put aside the hope of having the teaching prevail everywhere until the time of surging opportunity. For the time being, I wander about like a cloud or a waterweed and let the wind of the ancient sages be heard.

There may be true students who are not concerned with fame and gain, who allow their aspiration for enlightenment to guide them and earnestly desire to practice the buddha way. They may be misguided by incapable teachers and obstructed from the correct understanding, and, intoxicated in confusion, they may sink into the realm of delusion for a long time. How can they nourish the correct seed of prajñā and encounter the time of attaining the way? Since I am wandering about, which mountain or river can they call on? Because of my concern for them, I would like to record the standards of Zen monasteries, which I personally saw and heard in great Song, as well as the profound principle that has been transmitted by my master. I wish to leave for students of the way the authentic teaching of the buddha house. This is indeed the essence:

The great master Shākyamuni entrusted dharma to Mahā-kāshyapa at the assembly on Vulture Peak; it was then authentically transmitted from ancestor to ancestor down to Venerable Bodhidharma. Bodhidharma went to China and entrusted dharma to the great master Huike; this was the beginning of dharma transmission in the eastern country. In this way, by direct transmission, it reached Huineng, the Sixth Ancestor, Zen Master Dajian. Then the authentic buddha dharma spread in China, and the teaching that is not concerned with concepts and theories took form.

At that time there were two outstanding disciples of Huineng: Nanyue Huairang and Qingyuan Xingsi. They both equally received the Buddha's seal, as guiding masters of humans and devas. Their two lineages spread, and later the Five Gates opened: the Fayan School, the Guiyang School, the Caodong School, the Yunmen School, and the Linji School. At present in great Song China, only the Linji School prospers throughout the country. But in spite of their different styles, each of the Five Houses holds the one seal of the buddha mind.

In China after the Later Han dynasty [25–220 C.E.], the teachings of Buddhist scriptures were introduced and spread all over the land, but there was no conclusive teaching as yet. When Bodhidharma came from India [527 C.E.], the root of twining vines was immediately cut off, and the pure, single buddha dharma spread. Let us hope that it will be like this in our country.

Now, all ancestors and all buddhas who uphold buddha dharma have made it the true path of unfolding enlightenment to sit upright, practicing in the midst of receptive samādhi. Those who attained enlightenment in India and China followed this way. Thus, teachers and disciples intimately transmitted this excellent art as the essence of the teaching.

In the authentic tradition of our heritage, it is said that this directly transmitted, straightforward buddha dharma is the unsurpassable of the unsurpassable. From the first time you meet a master, without depending on incense offering, bowing, chanting buddha names, repentance, or reading scriptures, just wholeheartedly sit and thus drop away body and mind.

When even for a moment you sit upright in samādhi expressing the buddha mudrā [form] in the three activities [body, speech, and thought], the whole world of phenomena becomes the Buddha's mudrā and the entire sky turns into enlightenment. Accordingly, all buddha tathāgatas increase dharma bliss, the original source, and renew their magnificence in the awakening of the way. Furthermore, all beings in the world of phenomena in the ten directions and the six paths, including the three lower paths, at once obtain pure body and mind, realize the state of great emancipation, and manifest the original face. At this moment, all things actualize true awakening; myriad objects partake of the buddha body; and sitting upright, a glorious one under the bodhi tree, you immediately leap beyond the boundary of awakening. Then, you turn the unsurpassably great dharma wheel and expound the profound wisdom, ultimate and unconditioned.

This broad awakening comes back to you, and a path opens up to help you invisibly. Thus, in zazen you invariably drop away body and mind, cut through fragmented concepts and thoughts from the past, and realize essential buddha dharma. You cultivate buddha activity at innumerable practice places of buddha tathāgatas everywhere, provide the opportunity for everyone to engage in ongoing buddhahood, and vigorously uplift the dharma of going beyond buddha.

Because earth, grass, trees, walls, tiles, and pebbles of the world of phenomena in the ten directions all engage in buddha activity, those who receive the benefits of wind and water are inconceivably helped by the Buddha's transformation, splendid and unthinkable, and intimately manifest enlightenment. Those who receive these benefits of water and fire widely engage in circulating the Buddha's transformation based on original realization. Because of this, all those who live with you and speak with you also receive immeasurable buddha virtue, practice continuously, and extensively unfold the endless, unremitting, unthinkable, unnamable buddha dharma throughout the entire world of phenomena.

All this, however, does not appear within perception. Because it is unconstructedness in stillness, it is immediate realization. If practice and realization were two things, as it appears to an ordinary person, each could be recognized separately. But what can be met with recognition is not realization itself because realization is not reached with a discriminating mind.

In stillness, mind and object merge in realization and go beyond enlightenment. Thus, in the state of receptive samādhi, without disturbing its quality or moving a single particle, you engage in the vast buddha activity, the extremely profound and subtle buddha transformation.

Grasses, trees, and lands that are embraced by this way of transformation together radiate a great light and endlessly expound the inconceivable, profound dharma. Grass, trees, and walls bring forth the teaching to all beings, including common people and sages; all beings in response extend this dharma to grass, trees, and walls. Thus, the realm of self-awakening and awakening others invariably holds the mark of realization with nothing lacking, and realization itself is manifested without ceasing for a moment.

This being so, the zazen of even one person at one moment imperceptibly accords with all things and fully resonates through all time. Thus, in the past, future, and present of the limitless universe, this zazen carries on the Buddha's transformation endlessly and timelessly. Each moment of zazen is equally wholeness of practice, equally wholeness of realization.

This is so not only while sitting; like a hammer striking emptiness—before and after—its exquisite sound permeates everywhere. How can it be limited to this time and space? Myriad beings all manifest original practice, original face; it is impossible to measure.

Even if all buddhas of the ten directions, as innumerable as the sands of the Ganges, exert their strength and with the Buddha's wisdom try to measure the merit of one person's zazen, they will not be able to fully comprehend it.

ACTUALIZING THE FUNDAMENTAL POINT
Eihei Dōgen

AS ALL THINGS are buddha dharma, there are delusion, realization, practice, birth [life] and death, buddhas and sentient beings. As myriad things are without an abiding self, there is no delusion, no realization, no buddha, no sentient being, no birth and death. The buddha way, in essence, is leaping clear of abundance and lack; thus there are birth and death, delusion and realization, sentient beings and buddhas. Yet in attachment blossoms fall, and in aversion weeds spread.

To carry the self forward and illuminate myriad things is delusion. That myriad things come forth and illuminate the self is awakening.

Those who have great realization of delusion are buddhas; those who are greatly deluded about realization are sentient beings. Further, there are those who continue realizing beyond realization and those who are in delusion throughout delusion.

When buddhas are truly buddhas, they do not necessarily notice that they are buddhas. However, they are actualized buddhas, who go on actualizing buddha.

When you see forms or hear sounds, fully engaging body-and-mind, you intuit dharma intimately. Unlike things and their reflections in the mirror, and unlike the moon and its reflection in the water, when one side is illumined, the other side is dark.

To study the way of enlightenment is to study the self. To study the self is to forget the self. To forget the self is to be actualized by myriad things. When actualized by myriad things, your body and mind, as well as the bodies and minds of others, drop away.

No trace of enlightenment remains, and this no-trace continues endlessly.

When you first seek dharma, you imagine you are far away from its environs. At the moment when dharma is authentically transmitted, you are immediately your original self.

When you ride in a boat and watch the shore, you might assume that the shore is moving. But when you keep your eyes closely on the boat, you can see that the boat moves. Similarly, if you examine myriad things with a confused body and mind, you might suppose that your mind and essence are permanent. When you practice intimately and return to where you are, it will be clear that nothing at all has unchanging self.

Firewood becomes ash, and it does not become firewood again. Yet, do not suppose that the ash is after and the firewood before. Understand that firewood abides in its condition as firewood, which fully includes before and after, while it is independent of before and after. Ash abides in its condition as ash, which fully includes before and after. Just as firewood does not become firewood again after it is ash, you do not return to birth after death.

This being so, it is an established way in buddha dharma to deny that birth turns into death. Accordingly, birth is understood as beyond-birth. It is an unshakable teaching in the Buddha's discourse that death does not turn into birth. Accordingly, death is understood as beyond-death.

Birth is a condition complete this moment. Death is a condition complete this moment. They are like winter and spring. You do not call winter the beginning of spring, nor summer the end of spring.

Enlightenment is like the moon reflected on the water. The moon does not get wet, nor is the water broken. Although its light is wide and great, the moon is reflected even in a puddle an inch wide. The whole moon and the entire sky are reflected in dewdrops on the grass or even in one drop of water.

Enlightenment does not divide you, just as the moon does not break the water. You cannot hinder enlightenment, just as a drop of water does not crush the moon in the sky. The depth of the drop is the height of the moon. Each reflection, however long or short its duration, manifests the vastness of the dewdrop and realizes the limitlessness of the moonlight in the sky.

When dharma does not fill your whole body and mind, you may assume it is already sufficient. When dharma fills your body and mind, you understand that something is missing. For example, when you sail out in a boat to the middle of an ocean where no land is in sight and view the four directions, the ocean looks circular and does not look any other way. But the ocean is neither round nor square; its features are infinite in variety. It is like a palace. It is like a jewel. It only looks circular as far as you can see at that time. All things are like this.

Though there are many features in the dusty world and the world beyond conditions, you see and understand only what your eye of practice can reach. In order to learn the nature of the myriad things, you must know that although they may look round or square, the other features of oceans and mountains are infinite in variety; whole worlds are there. It is so not only around you, but also directly beneath your feet, or in a drop of water.

A fish swims in the ocean, and no matter how far it swims, there is no end to the water. A bird flies in the sky, and no matter how far it flies, there is no end to the air. However, the fish and the bird have never left their elements. When their activity is large, their field is large. When their need is small, their field is small. Thus, each of them totally covers its full range, and each of them totally experiences its realm. If the bird leaves the air, it will die at once. If the fish leaves the water, it will die at once.

Know that water is life and air is life. The bird is life and the fish is life. Life must be the bird and life must be the fish. You can go further. There is practice-enlightenment, which encompasses limited and unlimited life.

Now, if a bird or a fish tries to reach the end of its element before moving in it, this bird or this fish will not find its way or its place. When you find your place where you are, practice occurs, actualizing the fundamental point. When you find your way at this moment, practice occurs, actualizing the fundamental point, for the place, the way, is neither large nor small, neither yours nor others'. The place, the way, has not carried over from the past, and it is not merely arising now. Accordingly, in the practice-enlightenment of the buddha way, to attain one thing is to penetrate one thing; to meet one practice is to sustain one practice.

Here is the place; here the way unfolds. The boundary of realization is not distinct, for the realization comes forth simultaneously with the full experience of buddha dharma. Do not suppose that what you attain becomes your knowledge and is grasped by your intellect. Although actualized immediately, what is inconceivable may not be apparent. Its emergence is beyond your knowledge.

Mayu, Zen Master Baoche, was fanning himself. A monk approached and said, "Master, the nature of wind is permanent, and there is no place it does not reach. Why then do you fan yourself?"

"Although you understand that the nature of the wind is permanent," Mayu replied, "you do not understand the meaning of its reaching everywhere."

"What is the meaning of its reaching everywhere?" asked the monk again.

Mayu just kept fanning himself.

The monk bowed deeply.

The actualization of the buddha dharma, the vital path of its authentic transmission, is like this. If you say that you do not need to fan yourself because the nature of wind is permanent and you can have wind without fanning, you will understand neither permanence nor the nature of wind. The nature of wind is permanent; because of that, the wind of the Buddha's house brings forth the gold of the earth and ripens the cream of the long river.

觀世音
南無佛
與佛有因
與佛有緣
佛法僧緣
常樂我淨
朝念觀世音
暮念觀世音
念念從心起
念念不離心

PART FIVE

THE TEXTS ILLUMINATED

Daily Chants

(Audio track number at Shambhala.com/zenchants indicated where applicable)

AWAKENING TOGETHER *(Tracks 1 and 2)*

THIS VERSE IS widely chanted in Buddhist centers in East Asia. Traditionally it is used as the second part of the "Universal Dedication of Merit" or "Universal Transferring of Merit." (See p. 40, "Dedication.") Its ideographic title is 普回向—*Pu Huixiang* in Chinese and *Fu Ekō* in Japanese. However, this verse is also chanted by itself as an important reminder that one is meditating together with all the awakened ones and with all helpers for awakening from past, present, and future.

The ideographic version of this chant is

十方三世一切佛
至尊菩薩摩訶薩
摩訶般若波羅蜜

The common Japanese transliteration of this is

Ji hō san shi i shi fu.
Shi son bu sa mo ko sa.
Mo ko ho ja ho ro mi.

It is an ancient Sino-Japanese translation (based on the "Wu sound" of Chinese). Its later transliteration after the "Han sound," more understandable to the Japanese, although not commonly used for this verse, can be

Jippō sanze issai butsu
shison bosatsu makasatsu
maka hannya haramitsu.

A literal translation of this text is

Ten directions, three times, all buddhas
most venerable bodhisattva(s) mahāsattvas
mahā prajñā pāramitā.

A common translation is

All buddhas throughout space and time,
all bodhisattva mahāsattvas,
wisdom beyond wisdom—
mahā prajñā pāramitā.

This is a mere listing of nouns. But I have added "together may we realize," which is implied in the text. I believe it is still in the realm of translation.

In Japan, this text is chanted not only in the Zen School, but also the Shingon (Mantra) School and Nichiren School.

TERMS

ten directions: North, south, east, west, their midpoints, plus up and down.

three times: Past, present, and future.

bodhisattva: A Sanskrit word, literally "enlightenment being," who is committed to the awakening of others (see p.8).

buddha: An awakened or enlightened one. If not capitalized, it can mean any human being who is awakened. If capitalized, it can mean a historical or scriptural personality.

mahāsattva: Also a Sanskrit word, meaning "great being." In English, "bodhisattva mahāsattvas" is a common usage in Buddhist texts. In this case the former modifies the latter. In other words, *bodhisattva* and *mahāsattva* are described as the same being. If we say, however, *bodhisattvas mahāsattvas*, they can be different beings. In this way, we could venerate a number of great ones who are not usually regarded as bodhisattvas in the Buddhist context.

mahā pāramitā: In Sanskrit, means "great realization." *Pāramitā* means "arriving at the other shore of enlightenment." It is often translated as "perfection," but to me "realization" seems a more appropriate concept for our practice. In this line, the object of realization is not specified. But it seems that "prajñā" is implied as the object of realization.

CREDIT

A common translation, revised by Joan Halifax and modified by the Editor.

FOUR ALL-EMBRACING VOWS *(Tracks 3 and 4)*

This verse is called 四弘誓願文—*Si Hongshiyuan Wen* in Chinese and *Shi Guseigan Mon* in Japanese. In the Sōtō School it is called *Shi Kuseigan Mon*.

This verse, widely chanted by East Asian Buddhists, was put in its current form by Zhiyi (智顗 538–597), Liang to Sui dynasties, China—the founder of the Tiantai School.

Its ideographic version is

衆生無邊誓願度
煩惱無盡誓願斷
法門無量誓願學
佛道無上誓願成

Its Japanese transliteration is

Shujō muhen sei gan do.
Bonnō mujin sei gan dan.
Hōmon muryō sei gan gaku.
Butsudō mujō sei gan jō.

A common translation of this verse is

Sentient beings are numberless; I vow to save them.
Delusions are inexhaustible; I vow to end them.
Dharma gates are boundless; I vow to study them.
The buddha way is unsurpassable; I vow to attain it.

The version modified by Joan Halifax is

Creations are numberless; I vow to free them.
Delusions are inexhaustible; I vow to transform them.
Reality is boundless; I vow to perceive it.
The awakened way is unsurpassable; I vow to embody it.

It is sometimes explained that the four lines of this verse correspond to the four noble truths: the truth of suffering; the truth of the causes of suffering; the truth of the cessation of suffering; and the truth of the (eightfold) path. The eightfold path is wholesome view, wholesome thinking, wholesome speech, wholesome action, wholesome livelihood, wholesome effort, wholesome mindfulness, and wholesome samādhi (a Sanskrit word meaning "state of meditation").

TERMS

all-embracing: 弘—*hon* in Chinese and *gu* or *ku* in Japanese. It
means "broad," "extensive," and "far-reaching." This includes a
personal and universal vow.

beings: 衆生—*zhongsheng* in Chinese and *shujō* in Japanese—literally means "multitude of lives" or "many living beings."

awaken them: 度—*du* in Chinese and *do* in Japanese. It means
"crossing (them) across (to the shore of enlightenment through
the ocean of suffering)."

delusion: 煩惱—*fannao* in Chinese and *bonnō* in Japanese, which
comes from *klesha* in Sanskrit. Consisting of greed, hatred, and
ignorance.

end them: 斷—*duan* in Chinese and *dan* in Japanese. Literally
means "cut off."

dharma: A Sanskrit word, meaning "truth," "teaching," "thing," or
"phenomenon."

dharma gates: Aspects or characteristics of dharma.

CREDIT

A common translation, adapted by Joan Halifax, modified by the
Editor.

TEN-LINE LIFE-AFFIRMING SŪTRA OF AVALOKITESHVARA *(Tracks 5, 6, and 7)*

The title of this short scripture is 延命十句觀音經—*Yanming Shiju
Guanyin Jing* in Chinese and *Eimei Jikku Kannon Gyō* in Japanese.
Its ideographic version is

觀世音
南無佛
與佛有因

與佛有緣
佛法僧緣
常樂我淨
朝念觀世音
暮念觀世音
念念從心起
念念不離心

Its Japanese transliteration is

Kanzeon.
Namu butsu.
Yo butsu u in.
Yo butsu u en.
Buppōsō en.
Jō raku ga jō.
Chō nen Kanzeon.
Bo nen Kanzeon.
Nen nen jū shin ki.
Nen nen fu ri shin.

According to the *Chronology of Buddha Ancestors* (Fozu tongji), compiled by Zhipan in 1269 C.E., a defeated and imprisoned general, Wang Xuanmo (王玄謨), received this sūtra in a dream in 450 C.E., and the vigorous chanting of it saved his life from execution.

As Hakuin, the eighteenth-century Japanese Zen master of the Rinzai School, encouraged his students to chant it, this extrashort scripture has been chanted daily in Rinzai Zen monasteries and centers. It has also been recited in centers of the Sōtō School. The chanting becomes faster and louder while the verse is repeated.

Terms and Names

life-affirming: Literally means "life-prolonging."

Avalokiteshvara, perceiver of the cries of the world: The original name for the embodiment of compassion, 觀世音—Guanshiyin in Chinese and Kanze'on in Japanese, also abbreviated as 觀音, as in the title of the sutra—is a Chinese translation by Kumārajīva (鳩摩羅什 350–409). Its early original name in Sanskrit is Avaloki-tashvara. *Ava* means "down." *Lok* means "look" but has to do with *loka,* meaning "world." *Ashvara* means "unhappy voice." See p. 129 about the later name of this deity. *Avalokitashvara* is masculine in grammatical gender in Sanskrit but is described as having thirty-three incarnated bodies, including female ones, in the *Lotus Sūtra;* thus the deity became androgynous. In China, the belief that this deity is female developed around the tenth century. Thus it is commonly viewed that this deity is female in East Asia.

will be a buddha: The original phrase 與佛有因—*yu fo you yin* in Chinese and *yo butsu u in* in Japanese—literally means "for a buddha, having a cause." Having a cause to be awakened is to have aspiration and practice to be awakened.

helps all to awaken: The original phrase 與佛有縁—*yu fo you yuan* in Chinese and *yo butsu u en* in Japanese—literally means "for a buddha, have a condition." While a cause is a subjective element for a practitioner to be awakened, conditions are supporting elements, such as teachers, helpers, scriptures, and the environment for practice. It is implied in this that Avalokiteshvara is deter-mined to become a supporting condition for practitioners of dharma to be awakened.

be one with: The original word 念—*nian* in Chinese and *nen* in Japanese—literally means "thought," "moment," "mindful," or "intensely concentrate on."

moment by moment: The word 念—*nian* in Chinese and *nen* in

Japanese (same as above)—is repeated. In this case, each ideo-graph means "moment."

CREDIT
Translated by Joan Halifax and the Editor.

SŪTRA ON THE HEART OF REALIZING WISDOM BEYOND WISDOM *(Tracks 8 and 9)*

The *Heart Sūtra,* the most widely recited scripture in Mahāyāna Buddhism, summarizes in its brief form the selfless experience of reality in meditation, beyond our usual way of thinking. Its title is [摩訶]般若波羅蜜多心經—[*Mohe*] *Bore Boluomiduo Xinjing* in Chinese and [*Maka*] *Hannya Haramitta Shingyō* in Japanese. (The words in brackets in the title and text, in the currently chanted ver-sion, were later additions from an early Chinese version.)

The sūtra's ideographic version is

觀自在 菩薩　行深 般若波羅蜜多時　照見五蘊皆空
　　度 一切苦厄
舍利子　色不異空　空不異色　色即是空　空即是色
受想行識亦復如是
舍利子　是諸法空相　不生不滅不垢不淨不增不減
是故空中　無色無受想行識　無眼耳鼻舌身意
無色聲香味觸法　無眼界乃至無意識界
無無明亦無無明盡　乃至無老死亦無老死盡　無苦集滅道
無智亦無得　以無所得故　菩提薩埵依般若波羅蜜多
故心無罣礙無罣礙故　無有恐怖遠離 [一切] 顛倒夢想
究竟涅槃　三世諸佛　依般若波羅蜜多
故得阿耨多羅三藐三菩提
故知般若波羅蜜多　是大神咒　是大明咒　是無上咒
是無等等咒　能除一切苦　眞實不虚　故説般若波羅蜜多咒

即説咒曰　揭帝揭帝　般羅揭帝　般羅僧揭帝　菩提僧莎訶
般若波羅蜜多心經

Its Japanese transliteration is

Kan ji zai bo satsu gyō jin han nya ha ra mit ta ji
shō ken go on kai kū do is sai ku yaku
sha ri shi shiki fu i kū kū fu i shiki shiki soku ze kū
kū soku ze shiki ju sō gyō shiki yaku bu nyo ze
sha ri shi ze sho hō kū sō fu shō fu metsu fu ku fu jō fu
　　zō fu gen
ze ko kū chū mu shiki mu ju sō gyō shiki mu gen ni bi zes
　　shin ni
mu shiki shō kō mi soku hō mu gen kai nai shi mu i shiki kai
mu mu myō yaku mu mu myō jin nai shi mu rō shi yaku mu
　　rō shi jin
mu ku shū metsu dō mu chi yaku mu toku
i mu sho tok ko bo dai sat ta e han nya ha ra mit ta ko shin
　　mu kei ge
mu kei ge ko mu u ku fu on ri is sai ten dō mu sō
ku kyō ne han
san ze sho butsu e han nya ha ra mit ta
ko toku a noku ta ra sam myaku sam bo dai
ko chi han nya ha ra mit ta ze dai jin shu
ze dai myō shu ze mu jō shu ze mu tō dō shu nō jo is sai ku
shin jitsu fu ko ko setsu han nya ha ra mit ta shu soku setsu
　　shu watsu
gya tei gya tei ha ra gya tei hara sō gya tei bo ji sowa ka.
han nya shin gyō

This sūtra was translated from Sanskrit into Chinese in 649 by a
Chinese monk, Xuanzang (玄奘 602–664), a great translator who

journeyed alone to India and brought back many scriptures. An earlier Chinese version was given to Xuanzang, when he was studying in the western province of Shu around 622, by a sick monk. The text he was given, which I call the "α version," was not documented in any texts other than in a biography of Xuanzang by his students. That means there is no record that this sūtra was known or existed before the seventh century. The main part of this sūtra, however, coincides with a small segment of the *Mahā Prajñā Pāramitā Sūtra* (Kumārajīva's translation, completed in 405, of the *25,000-Line Prajñā Pāramitā* scripture, which emerged around the beginning of the Common Era).[7]

In my book *The Heart Sūtra: A Comprehensive Guide to the Classic in Mahayana Buddhism,* I endorsed the theory of the US scholar Jan Nattier that a Chinese version of the *Heart Sūtra* appeared before the Sanskrit version.

The Sanskrit title of the sūtra is *Prajñā Pāramitā Hridaya. Hridaya* means "heart," and *prajñā* means "transcendental wisdom." *Pāramitā,* originally meaning "having arrived (at the other shore)" is often translated as "perfection," but I prefer to translate it as "realizing" or "actualizing." My own definition of the "realization of wisdom beyond wisdom," which can be found in the above-mentioned book, is "a continuous, wholesome experience of freedom from and integrity in pluralistic and singularistic understanding and action."

The first English translation of the *Heart Sūtra* was done by Max Müller in 1881. D. T. Suzuki's translation, published in *Manual of Zen Buddhism* in 1950, has become the basis of a great number of later versions.

The version presented here is a new translation by Joan Halifax and me. Our intention for this translation is to bring forth the essential teaching of transcendence and freedom that is often obscured by seemingly negative and nihilistic expressions. We want to make the sūtra accessible to Buddhists as well as non-Buddhists, by replacing such traditional technical terms as *bodhisattva* and *nirvāna* with more easily understandable words.

The earlier and shorter version of the *Heart Sūtra* has been recited in the parts of the East Asian world that use ideographs. The later and longer version has been recited in the region of Vajrayāna Buddhism, in Tibetan and Mongolian. Our translation is based on the Chinese version by Xuanzang, which is the standard among shorter versions, in reference to its Sanskrit counterpart.

For a more detailed explanation of this sūtra, please see my book mentioned above.

TERMS AND NAMES

realizing wisdom beyond wisdom: See p. 9.

Avalokiteshvara: Sanskrit. *Ava* means "down." *Lok* means "look," "see," or "observe." *Lokita* is its past participle form. *Lokiteshvara* is a combination of *lokita* and *Īshvara. Īshvara,* meaning "Lord," is one of the one thousand titles of the Hindu deity Shiva.

five streams of body, mind, and heart: Five s*kandhas. Skandha* in Sanskrit means "aggregate," "heap," "division," or "path." Five skandhas are form (in this case "body"), feeling, perception, inclination (mental function that leads to voluntary and involuntary action), and discernment.

boundlessness: Shūnyatā in Sanskrit, meaning "zeroness." Commonly translated as "emptiness."

mantra: Sanskrit. A short mystic verse for incantation.

gaté, gaté . . . : A mantra is not usually translated but is sometimes interpreted. Thich Nhat Hanh interprets it as "Gone, gone, gone all the way over, everyone gone to the other shore, enlightenment, *svahā!*"[8] I interpret it "Arriving, arriving, arriving all the way, arriving together. Awakening. Svahā."

svahā: Sanskrit. Ancient Vedic sacred syllables, meaning "blessing" or "joy."

CREDIT

Translated by Joan Halifax and the Editor.

MEAL CHANT *(Track 10)*

This common meal chant is called "Five Reflections," 五観偈—
Wuguan Ji in Chinese and *Gokan no Ge* in Japanese. It is chanted
before formal and informal meals in the Mahāyāna tradition.

Its ideographic version is

一計功多少量彼來處
二忖己德行全缺應供
三防心離過貪等爲宗
四正事良藥爲療形枯
五爲成道故今受此食

Its Japanese translation in *kambun yomi*—a way to read Chinese
in Sino-Japanese with supplementary particles and changes in the
word sequences—is

Hitotsu ni wa, kō no tashō wo hakat te ka no raisho wo
    shiru.
Futatsu ni wa, onore no tokugyō no zenketsu wo hakat te
    ku ni ōzu.
Mittsu ni wa, shin wo fusegi ka wo hanaru ru wa ton tō
    wo shū to nasu.
Yottsu ni wa, masani ryōyaku wo koto to suru wa gyōko
    wo ryōze n ga tame nari.
Itsutsu ni wa, jōdō no tame no yue ni ima kono jiki wo uku.

Its literal translation is

One: we measure the amount of work and consider where
   it comes from.
Two: we reflect on our virtuous deeds, whether they are
   whole or lacking, and respond to the offering.
Three: we make it essential to protect our mind and depart
   from excess and greed, and the like.
Four: we indeed regard this food as good medicine to heal
   from withering (getting weak).
Five: we receive this food in order to attain the way.

I personally feel that this chant flows better without itemizing
numbers. So they are omitted in this version.

A slightly different version of this chant is mentioned in a commentary by Daoxuan (596–667) on the *Four-Part Precepts,* a collection of early Buddhist precepts.[9] Daoxuan is regarded as the
founder of the Nanshan Sect of the Precept School. Also, the exact
same text in ideography as above is found in Dōgen's "The Dharma
for Taking Food," written in 1246.[10]

Various Zen communities have developed shorter versions. One
by Joan Halifax is

> Earth, water, fire, air, and space combined to make this
> food. Numberless beings gave their lives and labors that
> we may eat. May we be nourished that we may nourish
> life.

The shortest version I know of is by Zen Master Dae Gak of Fur-
nace Mountain Zen Center, in Kentucky: "This food is universe."

CREDIT
A common translation, modified by the Editor.

This is a verse chanted before putting on a robe. A "robe" in this case means a *kesa* or a *rakusu* (in Japanese). A kesa—*kāshāya* in Sanskrit—is a formal patched robe worn over one shoulder by a Buddhist monk or nun. A *rakusu* is a simplified robe hung over the chest with a strap around the neck, worn by a home leaver or a layperson. This verse is chanted individually, and also communally, during a morning zazen period. Practitioners place a folded robe on their head and chant this verse before putting it on.

This verse is called 塔袈裟偈—*Ta Jiasha Ji* in Chinese, which is transliterated as *Takkesa Ge* in Japanese.

Its ideographic version is

大哉解脱服
無相福田衣
披奉如來教
廣度諸衆生

Its Japanese transliteration is

Dai sai gedappuku.
Musō fukuden e.
Hi bu nyorai kyō.
Kōdo shoshujō.

Eihei Dōgen (永平道元) wrote extensively on Buddhist robes in his essay "The Power of the Robe" in 1240 (included in *Treasury of the True Dharma Eye*). In this essay he reflects on his encounter with this verse when he first visited the Tiantong Monastery in China in 1223:

Once when I was in Song China, practicing on a long sitting platform, I observed the monks around me. At the beginning of zazen in the morning, they would hold up their kāshāyas, place them on their heads, and chant a verse quietly with palms together:

> Great is the robe of liberation,
> the robe of no form, the field of benefaction!
> I wear the Tathāgata's teaching
> to awaken countless beings.

This was the first time I had seen the kāshāya held up in this way and I rejoiced, tears wetting the collar of my robe. Although I had read this verse of veneration for the kāshāya in the Āgama Sūtra, I had not known the procedure. Now I saw it with my own eyes. In my joy I also felt sorry that there had been no master to teach this to me, and no good friend to recommend it in Japan. How sad that so much time had been wasted! But I also rejoiced in my wholesome past actions [that caused me to experience this]. If I had stayed in my land, how could I have sat side by side with the monks who had received and were wearing the buddha robe? My sadness and joy brought endless tears.

Then, I made a vow to myself: However unsuited I may be, I will become an authentic holder of the buddha dharma, receiving authentic transmission of the true dharma, and with compassion show the buddha ancestors' authentically transmitted dharma robes to those in my land.[11]

CREDIT
Translated by Blanche Hartman and the Editor, modified by Joan Halifax and the Editor.

THREE REFUGES *(Track 13)*

Some Zen communities in the West have started chanting this in Pali, the language that often carries earlier Buddhist teachings, commonly used in the Theravada tradition. Its translation is

> I take refuge in the Buddha.
> I take refuge in the dharma.
> I take refuge in the sangha.

> For the second time, I take refuge in the Buddha.
> For the second time, I take refuge in the dharma.
> For the second time, I take refuge in the sangha.

> For the third time, I take refuge in the Buddha.
> For the third time, I take refuge in the dharma.
> For the third time, I take refuge in the sangha.

For East Asian Buddhists, it is called 三歸依文— *San Quiyi Wen* in Chinese and *San Kie Mon* in Japanese.

The ideographic version of its first three lines is

> 南無歸依佛
> 南無歸依法
> 南無歸依僧

Its Japanese transliteration is

> Namu kie butsu.
> Namu kie hō.
> Namu kie sō.

TERMS

refuge: 南無—*namo* in Chinese and *namu* in Japanese—is a transliteration of the Sanskrit *namas,* meaning "taking refuge in." 歸依—*quiyi* in Chinese and *kie* in Japanese—is its translation, literally meaning "return and depend upon."

sangha: Sanskrit. Its ideographic transliteration, 僧伽—*sengga* in Chinese and *sōgya* in Japanese—is abbreviated as 僧 (*seng* in Chinese and *sō* in Japanese). A community of practitioners of dharma.

CREDIT

A common translation.

METTĀ (*Track 14*)

There are multiple versions of chants in Pali on the the theme of *mettā,* meaning "goodwill" or "loving-kindness." This chant is part of recitations called "The Sublime Attitude," along with *karunā* (compassion), *muditā* (empathetic joy), and *upekkhā* (equanimity). It is chanted at the Metta Forest Monastery, Valley Center, California, and is offered for use by the general public. It is translated as

> May I be happy.
> May I be free from stress and pain.
> May I be free from animosity.
> May I be free from oppression.
> May I be free from trouble.
> May I look after myself with ease.
>
> May all living beings be happy.
> May all living beings be free from animosity.
> May all living beings be free from oppression.

May all living beings be free from trouble.
May all living beings look after themselves with ease.

According to Dawn Neal, a researcher on mettā chants: Chanting for the meditator's own happiness such as "May I keep myself free from enmity, affliction and anxiety and live happily" is found in *Path of Purification* (Visuddhimagga), attributed to Theravada commentator Buddhaghosa of fifth century C.E. Sri Lanka. Buddhaghosa does not recommend that the practitioners simply focus on an aspiration that they themselves be happy or attempt absorption. Instead, the meditators are urged to use themselves as an example: "Just as I want to be happy and dread pain, as I want to live and not die, so do other beings, too."[12]

CREDIT
Translation by Thanissaro Bhikkhu.

GREAT COMPASSIONATE HEART DHĀRANĪ *(Track 15)*

The title of this mystic verse on Avalokiteshvara is 大悲心陀羅尼—*Dabei Xin Tuoluoni* in Chinese and *Daihi Shin Darani* in Japanese. The Buddha expounds the infinite magical benefits of this dhāranī in a short Vajrayāna Buddhist sūtra called 千手千眼觀世音菩薩廣大圓滿無礙大悲心陀羅尼經—*Qianshou Qianyan Guanshiyin Pusa Guangda Yuanman Wu'au Dabeixin Touluoni Jing* in Chinese and *Senju Sengen Kanzeon Bosatsu Kōdai Emman Muge Daihi Shin Darani Kyō* in Japanese.[13] The title of the sūtra can be translated as *One-Thousand-Arm, One-Thousand-Eye Avalokiteshvara Bodhisattva's Broad, Complete, Hindrance-Free, Great Compassionate Heart Dhāranī Sūtra.*

Its ideographic version is

南無喝 囉怛那哆囉夜耶 南無 阿唎耶婆盧羯帝爍鉢 囉耶

菩提薩跢婆耶 摩訶薩跢婆耶 摩訶迦盧尼迦耶

唵 薩皤囉罰曳數 怛那 怛寫 南無悉吉利埵 伊蒙

阿唎耶婆盧吉帝室佛囉㘄馱婆 南無 那囉謹墀醯唎

摩訶皤哆沙咩 薩婆阿他豆 輸朋 阿逝孕 薩婆薩哆那摩 婆伽摩
　　罰特豆

怛姪他 唵 阿婆盧醯 盧迦帝迦羅帝 夷醯唎 摩訶菩提薩埵

薩婆薩婆 摩羅 摩羅 摩醯摩醯 唎馱孕 俱盧俱盧 羯　懞度盧度盧

罰闍耶帝 摩訶罰闍耶帝 陀羅陀羅 地利尼室佛囉耶 遮羅遮羅

摩摩罰摩囉 穆帝囇 伊醯移醯 室那室那 阿囉嘇佛囉舍利

罰沙罰嘇 佛羅舍耶 呼嚧呼嚧摩囉呼嚧呼嚧 醯利 娑囉娑囉

悉利悉利 蘇嚧蘇嚧 菩提夜菩提夜 菩馱夜菩馱夜

彌帝利夜 那囉謹墀 地唎瑟尼那 波夜摩那娑婆訶 悉陀夜娑婆訶

摩訶悉陀夜娑婆訶 悉陀喩藝室皤囉耶娑婆訶 那囉謹墀娑婆訶

摩囉那囉娑婆訶 悉囉僧阿穆佉耶娑婆訶 娑婆摩訶阿悉陀夜娑
　　婆訶

者吉囉阿悉陀夜娑婆訶 波陀摩羯悉 哆夜娑婆訶 那囉謹墀皤伽囉
　　耶娑婆訶 摩婆利勝羯囉夜娑婆訶 南無喝囉怛那哆囉夜耶

南無阿唎耶婆嚧吉帝爍皤囉夜娑婆訶 悉殿都曼哆囉鉢馱耶
　　娑婆訶

The sūtra's earliest version is in the Vajrayāna Buddhist form of Sanskrit. Bhagavaddharma, a monk from western India, transliterated it into Chinese when he was in China between 650 and 655. The verse, chanted as a dhāranī, consists of eighty-two phrases and is formally called "Great Compassionate Heart Dhāranī of One-Thousand-Arm Avalokiteshvara." It is the essential part of the sūtra of that title translated by him.

The earliest guidelines for Zen monasteries, established by Baizhang Huaihai (百丈慧海, 749–814) of the Tang Dynasty, already mentioned chanting this dhāranī. The Sanskrit version was transliterated in Chinese by Amogavajra (705–774).

It is customary that dhāranīs are not translated or explained. Sometimes teachers of Esoteric Buddhism assert that chanting dhāranīs, which are beyond intellectual understanding, is an essential way to experience the indescribable heart of the Buddha. We present the Japanese way of reading this mystic verse.

For centuries, most Zen practitioners have been chanting this dhāranī without knowing its full meaning. But now we can, thanks to Shūyo Takubo, a Japanese scholar who restored the Sanskrit version of the "Great Compassionate Heart Dhāranī" from its Chinese and Japanese versions and decoded its original meaning.[14] Joan Halifax and I translated his Sanskrit version, which I include below.

> Homage to the three treasures.
> Homage to noble Avalokiteshvara, noble bodhisattva mahāsattva, who embodies great compassion.
> Om. Homage to you who protect all those who are fearful.
> Being one with you, the blue-necked noble Avalokiteshvara,
> I bring forth your radiant heart that grants all wishes, overcomes obstacles, and purifies delusion.
> Here is the mantra: Om. You are luminous with shining wisdom.
> You transcend the world.
> O, Lion King, great bodhisattva.
> Remember, remember, this heart.
> Act, act. Realize, realize. Continue, continue. Victor, great victor. Maintain, maintain. Embodiment of freedom.
> Arise, arise, the immaculate one, the undefiled being.
> Advance, advance. You are supreme on this earth.
> You remove the harm of greed.
> You remove the harm of hatred.
> You remove the harm of delusion.

Lion King, remove, remove all defilements.

The universal lotus grows from your navel.

Act, act. Cease, cease. Flow, flow. Awaken, awaken.

Compassionate one, enlighten, enlighten.

Blue-Necked One,

You bring joy to those who wish to see clearly. Svahā.

You succeed. Svahā. You greatly succeed. Svahā.

You have mastered the practice. Svahā.

Blue-Necked One. Svahā.

Boar-Faced One, Lion-Faced One. Svahā.

You, Holder of the Lotus. Svahā.

You, Holder of the Wheel. Svahā.

You liberate through the sound of the conch. Svahā.

You are the great Staff Bearer. Svahā.

You are the Destroyer of Darkness, abiding near the left
    shoulder. Svahā.

You, the Wearer of a Tiger Hide. Svahā.

Homage to the three treasures.

Homage to noble Avalokiteshvara. Svahā.

Realize all phrases of this mantra. Svahā.

Great Compassionate Heart Dāranī.

After we translated this, I realized that D. T. Suzuki had translated it and published it in 1950.[15]

Some of the phrases make reference to the Hindu god Shiva.
This fact suggests that Avalokiteshvara is originally related to
Shiva. In fact, Xuanzang, a great traveler and translator of seventh-
century China, reported in his *Record of the Western Regions Compiled during the Great Tang Dynasty:* "In the south of Mt. Malaya
on the southern end of India, there is a mountain called Potalaka,
where Avalokiteshvara visits and stays. When people pray to him,
he sometimes takes the form of Shiva or an ash-painted ascetic and

responds to their prayers."[16] In India to this day, there are devotees of Shiva, ascetics with their naked bodies covered with ash.

TERMS

three treasures: See p. 13.

oṃ: The Japanese transliteration of the Sanskrit word *oṃ*, a sacred sound of invocation.

svahā: See p. 129.

Blue-Necked One, Lion King, Destroyer of Darkness, Staff Bearer, Holder of the Wheel, Wearer of a Tiger Hide: Some of the one thousand names of Shiva.

the universal lotus grows from your navel: Based on the Hindu myth that Vishnu was lying on a coiled serpent in the waters of the void when a lotus stalk grew from his navel. The lotus blossomed to reveal Brahma, who sat on the flower and created heaven, earth, and all things.

CREDIT

A common Japanese transliteration.

WONDROUS AUSPICIOUS DHĀRAṆĪ FOR AVERTING CALAMITIES *(Track 16)*

The title for this mystic incantation is 消災妙吉祥陀羅尼—*Xiaozai Miao Jixian Tuoluoni* in Chinese and *Shōsai Myō Kichijō Darani* in Japanese. It is expounded in the sūtra called 佛説熾盛光大威德消災吉祥陀羅尼經—*Foshui Chicheng Daweide Xiaozai Tuoluoni Jing* in Chinese and *Bussetsu Shiseikō Dai'itoku Shōsai Kichijō Darani Kyō* in Japanese.[17] This title means "Expounded by the Buddha, Magnificent Light, Great, Mighty, Virtuous, Dissolving-Calamities, Auspicious Dhāraṇī Sūtra."

The original form of this mystic verse is, as in the preceding chant, in the Vajrayāna Buddhist form of Sanskrit. This dhāranī is the main part of a scripture called the *Sūtra on the Dhāranī of Glaring Light Great Awesome Merit of the Tathāgata Dissolving All Calamities*, translated into Chinese by Amogavajra (705–774), a renowned master of Vajrayāna, as well as one of the greatest Buddhist translators of the ideographic world in history.

Its ideographic version is

曩謨 三滿跢 沒馱喃 阿鉢囉賀哆舍娑娜喃 怛姪他 唵
佉佉 佉呬 佉呬 吽吽 入嚩囉入嚩囉 鉢囉入嚩攞鉢囉入嚩攞
底瑟姹底瑟姹 瑟致哩瑟致哩 薩普吒薩普吒 扇底迦室哩曳
娑嚩賀

This dhāranī is chanted daily in many Zen monasteries and groups.

Again, the meaning of this chant is usually not translated or explained. However, based on Shūyo Takubo's restored Sanskrit version, Jan Chozen Bays and I translated the Sanskrit version and present it here for your reference:[18]

> Homage to all buddhas—
> indestructible ones.
> O sacred, void, void.
> Clear away, clear away.
> Hum, hum.
> Shine, shine, shine brightly—
> stay, stay.
> Stars, stars, emerge, emerge.
> Peace and blessings.
> Svahā.

A common Japanese transliteration.

DEDICATION *(Tracks 20 and 21)*

This text, formally called "Universal Dedication of Merit" or "Universal Transference of Merit," usually precedes the verse "Awakening Together," which I presented at the beginning of this book. Its title in ideography is 普回向—*Pu Huixiang* in Chinese and *Fu Ekō* in Japanese. *Huixiang,* or *ekō,* literally means "to turn around and direct," indicating that one turns around the benefit received by one's practice of dharma and extends the benefit to others. This is chanted at the end of daily chanting and in ceremonies in such Japanese schools as Tendai, Shingon, Zen, and Nichiren.

The text in ideography is

願以此功德
普及一切
我等與衆生
皆共成佛道

In Japanese it is read in *kambun yomi.*

Negawa ku wa kono kudoku wo mot te
amaneku issai ni oyobo shi
warera to shujō tozen
mina tomo ni butsudō wo jōze n koto wo.

This text in Chinese comes from "Miraculous Palaces," chapter 7, fascicle 3, of the *Lotus Sūtra,* translated by Kumārajīva from Sanskrit into Chinese in 406. (In the Sanskrit version, this chapter is titled "Pūvayoga," or "Practice in the Past Life.") In this chapter, numerous forms of the god Brahma see a great many palaces and towers illuminating and sparkling. They offer them to the Buddha and praise him in a verse, which is concluded with this dedication.

Credit

A common translation, modified by the Editor.

BUDDHA ANCESTORS *(Track 17 and 18)*

This chant is called 佛祖名號—*Fozu Minghao* in Chinese and *Busso Myōgō* in Japanese.

Some practitioners don't like to chant this line of only male teachers. Agreeing with them, I have been suggesting to place "Prajñā Pāramitā, Mother of All Buddhas" at the beginning of the list, in a small way recognizing that this vast and deep teaching could not have come to us only through men.

This list of ancestors consists of seven original buddhas (six mythological buddhas plus the historical Shākyamuni Buddha), legendary Indian masters, Chinese masters, and early Japanese masters. The Sixth Chinese Ancestor, Dajian Huineng (大鑑慧能), had successors, including Nanyue Huairang (南嶽懷讓) and Qingyuan Xingsi (青原行思), from whom the Nanyue Line and Qingyuan Line started, soon diverging into the Five Schools of Zen, including the Linji School and Caodong School.

The Japanese Rinzai and Sōtō Schools are descendants of these lineages. All current dharma holders of the Rinzai School are descendants of Hakuin Ekaku (白隠慧鶴, 1685–1768), the reformer of the school, who carried the lineage of Nampo Shōmyō (1235–1308), in the left column on page 42. (Myōan Eisai 明庵榮西, the founder of the Rinzai School, came from a line that diverged from Huanglong Huinan and Xu'an Huaichang.) If you are in the lineage of the Rinzai School, you recite names from the beginning and diverge into the left column, followed by names of masters up to your own teacher.

All dharma holders of the Sōtō School come from Dōgen's lineage, in the right column, through Keizan Jōkin, followed by generations of masters up to your own teacher.

Terms and Names

Vipashin Buddha, . . . : The names of the seven original buddhas—six mythological buddhas plus Shākyamuni Buddha—are sometimes given with meanings. They are Vipashin (Boundless Discourse), Shikhin (Fire), Vishvabhū (Universal Compassion), Krakucchanda (Gold Wizard), Kanakamuni (Golden Sage), Kāshyapa (Drinking Light), and Shākyamuni (Patient Silence).

ancestors: Teachers and their teachers in the lineage of a practitioner.

Credit

A common translation, revised by the Editor.

FEMALE BUDDHA ANCESTORS *(Track 19)*

There have been a great number of female Zen practitioners and teachers, but few of them have been recognized while others have been forgotten or not mentioned. The attempts to create lists of female buddha ancestors, which seem to have started recently in the United States based on feminist spirituality, are admirable. In these lists the names have been taken from Buddhist scriptures, Chinese and Japanese Zen texts, historical records, and personal affinity. The list presented in this book owes much to an effort by Grace Schireson assembling it in collaboration with other scholars and practitioners. Originally called "Women Ancestors," this list was approved by a committee at the Sōtō Zen Buddhist Association in the United States in 2010.

The list consists of mystic figures, ancient Indian teachers and practitioners, followed by Chinese and Japanese, and concludes with teachers and a practitioner (Baihō Trudy Dixon) who were active in the United States. In contrast to the traditionally established lineage-based Zen ancestors, the emerging lists of female buddha ancestors are nonsectarian, nonlinear, and flexible so that every Zen community may develop its own version to suit the preference of its members. As the selection process has just started, scholarship needs to develop, and selections are yet to be refined.[19]

CREDIT
Sōtō Zen Buddhist Association version compiled by Grace Shireson; renamed by the Editor.

ATONEMENT

This verse comes from "Samantabhadra's Vows," chapter 40 of the *Avatamsaka Sūtra* (of which the title can be translated as "Flower Splendor Sūtra"), which was first translated from Sanskrit into Chinese by Buddhabhadra in 419 to 420.[20] It is called "Repentance Verse." Its title in ideography is 懺悔文—*Chuahui Wen* in Chinese and *Sange Mon* in Japanese. It is also called "Simplified Repentance," 略懺悔—*Lue Chuahui* in Chinese and *Ryaku Sange* in Japanese.

Its ideographic version is

我昔所造諸惡業
皆由無始貪瞋痴
從身語意之所生
一切我今皆懺悔

There are slightly varied translations, one of which is

All my ancient twisted karma
from beginningless greed, hate, and delusion
born of body, speech, and mind—
I now fully avow.

This text is widely chanted in Mahāyāna Buddhism during ordination and monthly repentance ceremonies on full-moon evenings.

A human being is a compound of innumerable causes and effects. Each one of us is here in this world because of many decisions made by our parents and their parents, all the way from the beginning of time. Our upbringing is the result of biological elements, history, culture, social conditions, personality, education, and many other events that happened in the past and are happening in the present. We are the visible and invisible effect of limitless karma—individual and collective social actions.

Thus, we are influenced by a tremendous amount of forces that are completely out of our control. Under these limitations, however, there are also a great number of elements we can control and change. Changing one's gender, nationality, religion, or legal name is not easy, but it is not impossible, either. Changing one's partner, career, diet, exercise, tastes, habits, behavior, way of thinking, way of speaking, lifestyle, and daily schedule is possible. We are in the midst of changeable and unchangeable karma in each moment. We are bound by cause and effect, but at the same time we are partly free of cause and effect. This is the case during meditation, when we can be completely free from the chain of causation. At this time, we can be anybody and anywhere. We are what we meditate. We are also the source of cause and effect.

Looking at all existing translations so far, including the version above, gives me an impression that people atone only "ancient" twisted karma, and not the recent or current karma. But we also need to atone recent and current unwholesome actions, a need that is reflected in the translation I present.

Terms

karma: Sanskrit. Action and its visible and invisible result. But it often implies the result of unwholesome action. The ideographs 惡業—*eye* in Chinese and *akugō* in Japanese—in the first line of the original chant literally mean "bad karma" or "evil karma."

Credit

A common translation, revised by the Editor.

REMINDER

This verse is called 版偈—*Ban Ji* in Chinese and *Han Ge* in Japanese. Its ideographic version is

生死事大
無常迅速
各宜醒覺
慎勿放逸

This phrase is written, in its entirety or partly, on a wooden sounding board, called *han* in Japanese, which is hung near the Zen meditation hall and hit by a wooden mallet for signaling zazen. There is an illustration of a han with this phrase in the monastic guidelines for the Ōbaku monasteries written by Ingen Ryūki (隠元隆琦; Chinese pronunciation: Yinyuan Longqi), 1592–1673, a Chinese monk who founded the Ōbaku School of Zen in Edo-period Japan. The Ōbaku School is in the lineage of Huangbo Xiyun (黃檗希運, d. 850), the teacher of Linji Yixuan (臨濟義玄, d. 867).

It is recited by the one who hits the han. In some Western Zen monasteries, the chant leader recites this verse at the end of the evening sitting period.

CREDIT
A common translation, modified by the Editor.

CHANTS FOR EVENTS

OPENING THE SŪTRA VERSE

THIS VERSE IS widely chanted in Mahāyāna Buddhism before reciting a sūtra in ceremony or while opening a sūtra book. It is also recited before a dharma talk. Its title in ideography is 開經偈—*Kaijing Ji* in Chinese and *Kaikyō Ge* in Japanese. Its ideographic expression is

無上甚深微妙法
百千萬劫難遭遇
我今見聞得受持
願解如來眞實義

In Japanese it is sometimes chanted in Sino-Japanese pronunciation:

Mujō jinjin mimyō hō
hyaku sen man gō nan sōgū.
Ga kon kemmon toku juji.
Gange nyorai shinjitsu gi.

It is also chanted in *kambun yomi*—Sino-Japanese pronunciation grammatically modified with a mixture of indigenous Japanese pronunciations:

Mujō jinjin mimyō no hō wa
hyaku sen man gō ni mo aiai gata shi.

Ware ima kemmon shi jujisuru koto wo e tari.
Negawaku wa nyorai no shijitsu gi wo ese n koto wo.

The author of this chant is unknown. It was already mentioned by Nichiren (日蓮, 1222–1282), the founder of the Nichiren School in Japan, in his book *Outline of the Lifetime Sacred Teaching* (Ichidai Shōgyō Taii).

Thich Nhat Hanh translated this verse as

The Dharma is deep and lovely.
We now have a chance to see it,
study it, and practice it.
We vow to realize its true meaning.[21]

CREDIT
A common translation, modified by the Editor.

VERSE FOR HEARING THE MALLET

This verse is chanted before setting out bowls in formal meals in Zen monasteries or in Zen intensive retreats. Upon hearing the first sounding signal, the practitioners chant this verse. In front of them is a cloth wrapping, inside of which are three bowls, a pair of chopsticks, a spoon, a bowl swab, a dishcloth, and a napkin. This set of bowls and utensils is called *ōryōki* in Japanese. This text is called "Verse on Hearing the Mallet," 聞槌偈—*Wenchui Ji* in Chinese and *Montsui Ge* in Japanese.

Its ideographic version is

佛生迦毘羅
成道摩掲陀

説法波羅奈
入滅拘絺羅

Dōgen does not mention this verse in "The Dharma for Taking
Food." But Ingen Ryūki (see p. 147) mentions it in his *Pure Guidelines for the Ōbaku School* (Ōbaku Shingi), published in 1672.[22]

TERMS AND NAMES
ōryōki: A Japanese word, meaning "utensils for a suited amount."
   ("Utensils" here include bowls.)
Kapilavastu: Literally, town of Kapila, center for the Shākya Clan's
   region (present-day central southern Nepal, bordering India).
   Lumbinī Garden, where Prince Siddhārtha (later Shākyamuni
   Buddha) was born, is in the western side of the town. Siddhārtha's father, King Shuddodana, ruled this region.
Magadha: An ancient kingdom of northeastern India, currently
   southern Bihār, bordering Nepal. Buddha Gaya, where Shākyamuni Buddha was enlightened, is located in this region, and
   much of his dharma discourses, later recorded in scriptures, took
   place on Vulture Peak, near its capital city, Rājagriha.
Vārānasī: City on the Ganges in central northern India. The Buddha gave his first dharma discourse in Deer Park there. Capital
   city of the ancient kingdom of Kāshi. The most sacred center of
   Brahmanism/Hinduism.
Kushinagara: A town in the north of the kingdom of Magadha,
   where the Buddha's *pari-nirvāna* took place.

CREDIT
A common translation, modified by the Editor.

SETTING OUT THE BOWLS

Traditionally, the practitioners unwrap the bowls and utensils, setting them out in a ritualized way, while chanting this verse. But it can also be chanted before the bowls are set out. This is called 展鉢偈—*Zhanbo Ji* in Chinese and *Tempatsu Ge* in Japanese.

Its ideographic version is

如來應量器
我今得敷展
願共一切衆
等三輪空寂

Dōgen does not mention this verse in his detailed instruction "The Dharma for Taking Food." It is found in *Daily Guidelines for Assembly Joiners* (Ruzong Riyong Qiqui) by the Zen master Wuliang Zongshou (無量宗壽) of China, presented in 1209.[23]

TERMS

Tathāgata: A Sanskrit word—an honorific title of the Buddha, meaning "one who has thus come" or "one who has come from thusness."

three wheels: In this case, the dynamically ongoing relations among the giver, the receiver, and the gift.

be liberated: The last compound, *kūjaku* 空寂, can be interpreted as "empty and serene" or "boundless (interconnected) and in profound serenity (nirvāna)" or "in a nondual state."

CREDIT

A common translation, modified by the Editor.

INVOCATION

After the bowls are set on the meal board for a formal meal, the names of deities are chanted. This is called "Ten Buddha Names," 十佛名—*Shifo Ming* in Chinese and *Jūbutsu Myō* in Japanese.

Its version in ideography is

清浄法身毘盧遮那佛
圓満報身盧遮那佛
千百億化身釋迦牟尼佛
當來下生彌勒尊佛
十方三世一切諸佛
大乘妙法蓮華經
大聖文珠殊利菩薩
大乘普賢菩薩
大悲觀世音菩薩
諸尊菩薩摩訶薩
摩訶般若波羅蜜

"Buddha" is an awakened one, and "bodhisattva" is one who helps others to awaken, but, as in the case of "Ten Buddha Names," "buddhas" means deified beings that include bodhisattvas.

Dōgen lists these names in his guideline "The Dharma for Taking Food."[24] He also indicates that this invocation is chanted at the beginning of a three-month practice period.[25] Already in his time, the list included eleven names, just as it does now. It is possible that the last name on the list, "Mahā Prajñā Pāramitā," is not regarded as a buddha or bodhisattva, but as the "profound realization of wisdom beyond wisdom" of these deities, and perhaps of the chanters.

TERMS AND NAMES

dharmakāya: The dharma body that is the absolute aspect of truth, equal to the whole universe of phenomena. It is one aspect of the threefold body (*kāya* in Sanskrit) of Buddha Shākyamuni in the Mahāyāna pantheon, along with *sambhogakāya* and *nirmānakāya.*

Vairochana Buddha: The manifestation of the reality of the universe, literally meaning "Illumination Buddha."

sambhogakāya: The reward body that is also an enjoyment, bliss, or purified body, associated with the fruit of practice.

Rochana Buddha: Regarded as another name of Vairochana.

nirmānakāya: The manifestation body that appears in the world and acts for the benefit of beings. Shākyamuni Buddha, in this case, is regarded as having hundreds, thousands, and millions of incarnated bodies.

Maitreya Buddha: Predicted to come down as the next buddha from Tushita Heaven to the continent of Jambudvīpa—where the human world is—and awaken those who will have missed the teaching of Shākyamuni Buddha. This will take place 5,670,000,000 years in the future.

Saddharma Pundarīka Sūtra: The *Sūtra of Wondrous White Lotus Dharma,* often regarded as the king of all sūtras in Mahāyāna Buddhism.

Mañjushrī: Bodhisattva of wisdom, whose figure is often enshrined in the center of a meditation hall.

Samantabhadra: Bodhisattva of awakened practice. An image of this bodhisattva, along with that of Mañjushrī, often accompanies that of Shākyamuni Buddha.

CREDIT

A common transliteration, modified by the Editor.

OFFERING FOOD FOR SPIRITS

This chant is called "Verse of Rice for Beings," 生飯偈—*Shengfan Ji* in Chinese and *Saba Ge* in Japanese.

Before the midday formal meal, practitioners put a small amount of rice on the handle of the bowl swab, put their palms together, and chant this verse.

Its ideographic version is

汝等鬼神衆

我今施汝供

此食偏十方

一切鬼神共

Its reading in Japanese is

Ji ten ki jin shu

go san su ji kyū

su ji hen ji hō

i shi ki jin kyū.

Both the title and the chant reflect an ancient transliteration of the ideographs.

Dōgen describes the procedure of offering food at midday meals in "The Dharma of Taking Food" but does not mention this verse.

This verse is found in chapter 16 of the *Mahā Pari-nirvāna Sūtra*.[26] The scripture tells the story that originated this custom: After a ghost in the wilderness took the precept of not killing, he starved for not having eaten meat. The Buddha saw it and told one of his disciples to offer food to the ghost at each meal.

TERMS

rice for beings: 牛飯—*shengfan* in Chinese and *saba* in Japanese. *Sheng,* or *sa,* means "life" but in this context "living being(s)" or "sentient being(s)." This term sometimes means "unawakened being(s)," in contrast with "awakened being(s)." *Fan,* or *ba,* means "cooked rice" or "meal."

spirits: A translation of 鬼神衆—*guishen zhong* in Chinese and *kijin shu* in Japanese, literally meaning "(hungry) ghosts and (other) spirits."

CREDIT

A common translation, modified by the Editor.

RAISING THE BOWL

After the food is served and before eating, the practitioners raise the first (largest) bowl, called the "Buddha bowl," with both hands and chant this dedication. It is called "Verse for Bowl Raising," 擎鉢文—*Qingbo Wen* in Chinese and *Keihatsu Mon* in Japanese.

Its ideographic version is

上分三寳
中分四恩
下及六道
皆同供養
一口爲斷一切悪
二口爲修一切善
三口爲度諸衆生
皆共成佛道

Dōgen does not mention this chant in "The Dharma of Taking Food." But this is found in *Guidelines for the Zen Monasteries,* the oldest extant collections of monastic guidelines, compiled by Changlu Zongze (長蘆宗賾) of the Yunmen School, published in 1103 in China.[27]

TERMS

three treasures: Buddha, dharma, and sangha—the enlightened one, truth or teaching, and the community of practitioners of dharma.

four benefactors: In a common classification these are parents, sentient beings, the king, and the three treasures.

six paths: The six destinations in the cycle of birth, death, and rebirth —the realms of devas (gods or celestial beings), human beings, fighting spirits (*asuras*), animals, hungry ghosts, and hell beings.

first portion . . . : I find Griffith Foulk's explanation of the three portions very helpful. He says: "The designations 'upper' (*jō*, 上), 'middle' (*chū*, 中), and 'lower' (*ge*, 下) invite one to imagine three separate portions (*bun*, 分) in what is actually a single bowl filled with rice; the point is that portions are offered 'up' to worship and honor superior beings, 'across' as thanks to those of equal status who have provided help, and 'down' to pitiable beings in unhappy rebirths who need help."[28]

CREDIT

Common translation, modified by the Editor.

OFFERING RINSE WATER

After eating during the formal meal, practitioners rinse their chopsticks, spoon, and bowls with distributed water, drink some, and offer the rest for spirits. This verse is called "Verse for Sharing Water," 折水偈—*Sheshui Ji* in Chinese and *Sessui no Ge* in Japanese. This chant reflects a teaching that even gray water is precious and can be a gift to those who benefit from it.

Its ideographic version is

我此洗鉢水
如天甘露味
施與鬼神衆
悉令得飽満
唵摩休羅細娑婆訶

Its reading in Japanese is

Ga shi sen has sui
nyo ten kan ro mi
se yo ki jin shu
shitsu ryō toku bō man
om ma ku ra sai so waka.

Again, Dōgen does not mention this verse in "the Dharma of Taking Food." A slightly different version is found in *Pure Guidelines for the Ōbaku School*, mentioned above.[29]

TERMS

Om ma ku ra sai so wa ka: A mantra. "Om" (a phonetically changed form of "on") is the Japanese transliteration of the Sanskrit word *oṃ,* a sacred sound of invocation. "Ma ku ra sai" represents the Sanskrit word *Maheshvara,* which can be broken down as *Mahā Īshvara,* meaning "Great Lord." It is the name of the Hindu deity Shiva, assimilated into Buddhism. "So wa ka" is, as in the *Heart Sutra* mantra, *svahā* in Sanskrit, meaning "blessing!"[30]

CREDIT

A common translation, modified by the Editor.

VERSE OF PURE PRACTICE

To conclude the formal meal, the head chanter recites the "Verse of Pure Practice While Abiding in the World." Its ideographic name is 處世界梵偈—*Chu Shiga Fan Ji* in Chinese and *Sho Sekai Bon no Ge* in Japanese. *Fan,* or *bon,* is a transliteration of the Sanskrit word *brahma,* meaning, in this case, "practice of purity" or "observing precepts." The text in ideography is

處世界如虛空
如蓮花不著水
心清淨超於彼
稽首禮無上尊

Its literal translation is "Placed in the world like empty sky, like a lotus blossom not touching the water, the mind is pure and beyond that (water); I (we) vow to the unsurpassable honorable one."

This is based on a common analogy that the purity of a dharma practitioner living in the world full of defilement should be like a lotus plant on a stem, rooted in muddy water but blooming in the air above the water.

The first compound of the last line—*keishu,* 稽首—literally means to "bow to." But the intention of this chant seems to carry better if we say "(we) follow."

This verse is found in a description of the procedure for a novice ordination, fascicle 9, of *Guidelines for the Zen Monasteries* (Chan-yuan Qinggui), compiled by Changlu Zongze. It was published in 1103—the oldest extant collection of monastic guidelines.[31]

CREDIT
A common translation, revised by the Editor.

UNIVERSAL PRECEPTS OF THE SEVEN ORIGINAL BUDDHAS

Its title in ideography is 七佛通戒偈—*Qifo Tongjie Ji* in Chinese and *Shichibutsu Tsūkai no Ge* in Japanese. Its text in ideography is

諸悪莫作
衆善奉行
自淨其意
是諸佛教

This phrase is found in chapter 14 of the Chinese translation of the Sanskrit sūtra, *Dharmapada*.[32] Its Pali version is *Dhammapada,* regarded as a scripture that contains the earliest teachings of the Buddha. As a summary of the entire Buddhist teaching, this verse is widely chanted by Buddhists in general.

The seven original buddhas, often referred to as the "seven buddhas in the past," are, as shown in "Buddha Ancestors" (p. 41), the six mystical buddhas and the historical Shākyamuni Buddha.

Dōgen wrote an essay called "Refrain from Unwholesome Action" (Shoaku Makusa), in 1240, as a part of his lifework *Treasury of the True Dharma Eye* (Shōbō Genzō).[33] The title of the essay is taken from the first line of this universal precept.

TERMS

unwholesome: The ideograph 悪—*e* in Chinese and *aku* in Japanese—is sometimes translated as "evil," but my cotranslator, Mel Weitsman, chose the term "unwholesome." "Evil" may imply extremely bad actions, like murdering, without taking into account common mistakes like speaking ill of others, which the ten prohibitory precepts warn against.

CREDIT

A common translation, revised by Mel Weitsman and the Editor.

MAINTAINING THE PRECEPTS

The vows to maintain the precepts are recited during ceremonies, including the repentance ceremony that takes place on the day of the full moon.

The process for giving and receiving precepts is elucidated by Dōgen in his undated essay "Receiving the Precepts" in his *Treasury of the True Dharma Eye*.[34] The main part of the ceremony is a dialogue by the officiant and the recipient(s) of the precepts:

> [the officiant says:]
> Good person. You have given up incorrect views and taken refuge in the true teaching. The precepts surround you.
> Now, take the three universal pure precepts.
> One: the precept of observing guidelines.
> Will you maintain this precept from now until you attain a buddha body?
> [the recipient says:]
> Yes, I will maintain it.
> [the officiant says:]
> Please maintain it.

On each of the three universal pure precepts and the ten prohibitory precepts, this dialogue takes place.

The ideographic versions of these precepts are

攝律儀戒
攝善法戒
饒益眾生戒

不殺生
不偷盗
不貧婬
不妄語
不酤酒
不説在家出家菩薩罪過
不自讚毀他
不慳法財
不瞋恚
不癡謗三寶

These precepts can still stand nowadays as they existed in Dōgen's times, except for the fifth prohibitory precept, "Not to buy or sell alcohol." See below.

TERMS

use intoxicants: The earlier precept says "not to sell or buy alcohol." "Not to use intoxicants" is a contemporary Western adaptation of this precept.

not to speak of the faults of others: The ideographic version says, "Not to speak of the faults of lay and home-leaver bodhisattvas."

CREDIT

A common translation and adaptation.

ADMONITION

This text, written in 1335, is known in Japanese as 興禅大燈國師遺戒—*Kōzen Daitō Kokushi Yuikai* (Last Admonition of National Teacher Kōzen Daitō). The ordination name of the author is Shūhō Myōchō (宗峰妙超, 1282–1337), who lived during the Kamakura and Muromachi periods. He practiced Rinzai Zen and became a dharma heir of Nampo Shōmyō.[35]

According to folklore, when Emperor Hanazono wanted to see Myōchō, no one could tell who he was among the crowd of beggars under a bridge in the capital city of Kyōto. The officer who was ordered to search for him learned that Myōchō loved melon. So he said to the beggars, "Come without a foot and get it." One of them replied, "Give it without a hand!" In this way, Myōchō was caught and taken before the emperor. The emperor said, "How auspicious—the Buddha's law meets the king's law." Myōchō said, "How auspicious—the king's law meets the Buddha's law." Deeply impressed, the emperor asked Myōchō to be his teacher and later honored him with the title "National Teacher Kōzen Daitō."

Myōchō became abbot of the Daitoku Monastery, one even higher than the Five Mountains, the top-ranking Zen monasteries of Japan. He is regarded as the founder of the Daitoku-ji Sect of the Rinzai School. This admonition is chanted daily in Rinzai monasteries.

Its original text—a mixture of ideographs and phonetics—is

汝ら諸人この山中に来
道の為に頭をあつむ
佛道衣食の爲にすること莫れ
肩あって着ずということなく
口あって食らわずということなし
ただ須らく十二時中無理會の處に向って
窮め来り究め去るべし
光陰矢の如慎んで雑用心すること勿れ
看取せよ看取せよ
老僧行脚の後或は寺門繁興し
佛閣經卷に金銀をちりばめ多衆囂熱

或いは誦經諷咒長坐不臥一食卯斎六時行

直饒恁麼にし去るといえども

佛祖不傳の妙道を以て胸間に掛在せずんば

則ち因果を撥無し眞風地に堕つ

併なこれ邪魔の種族なり

老僧世を去ること久しくとも兒孫と稱することを許さず

或は儻し一人あり野外に綿絶し一把茅底折脚鐺内に

野菜根を煮て喫して日を過すとも專一に己事を究明する者は

老僧と日日相見報恩底の人也

誰か敢えて軽忽せんや勉旃勉旃

CREDIT

Translated by Peter Levitt and the Editor.

ENLIGHTENMENT POEMS

ENGRAVING TRUST IN THE HEART

THE TITLE of this poem is 信心銘—*Xinxin Ming* in Chinese and *Shinjin Mei* in Japanese. This text is included in the *Jingde Record of Transmission of the Lamp,* compiled by Yong'an Daoyuan (永安道原) in 1004.[36]

This verse is attributed to Jianzhi Sengcan (鑑智僧璨 d. 606), of the early Tang dynasty, the Third Chinese Ancestor of the Chan, or Zen, School. The earliest known commentary on this verse was written by Zhenxie Qingle (眞歇清了 1089–1151) of the Caodong School.

Its ideographic version is

至道無難	唯嫌揀擇	但莫憎愛	洞然明白	毫釐有差
天地懸隔	欲得現前	莫存順逆	違順相爭	是爲心病
不識玄旨	徒勞念靜	圓同太虛	無欠無餘	良由取捨
所以不如	莫逐有緣	勿住空忍	一種平懷	泯然自盡
止動歸止	止更彌動	唯滯兩邊	寧知一種	一種不通
兩處失功	遣有沒有	從空背空	多言多慮	轉不相應
絕言絕慮	歸根得旨	隨照失宗	須臾返照	勝却前空
前空轉變	皆由妄見	不用求眞	唯須息見	二見不住
愼勿追尋	纔有是非	紛然失心	二由一有	一亦莫守
一心不生	萬法無咎	無咎無法	不生不心	能隨境滅
境逐能沈	境由能境	能由境能	欲知兩段	元是一空
一空同兩	齊含萬像	不見精麁	寧有偏黨	大道體寬
無易無難	小見狐疑	轉急轉遲	執之失度	心入邪路
放之自然	體無去住	任性合道	逍遙絕惱	繫念乖眞

沈惛不好　不好勞神　何用疎親　欲趣一乘　勿惡六塵
六塵不惡　還同正覺　智者無爲　愚人自縛　法無異法
妄自愛著　將心用心　豈非大錯　迷生寂亂　悟無好惡
一切二邊　妄自斟酌　夢幻空華　何勞把捉　得失是非
一時放却　眼若不眠　諸夢自除　心若不異　萬法一如
一如體玄　兀爾忘緣　萬法齊觀　歸復自然　泯其所以
不可方比　止動無動　動止無止　兩既不成　一何有爾
究竟窮極　不存軌則　啓心平等　所作俱息　狐疑盡淨
正信調直　一切不留　無可記憶　虛明自然　不勞心力
非思量處　識情難測　眞如法界　無他無自　要急相應
唯言不二　不二皆同　無不包容　十方智者　皆入此宗
宗非促延　一念萬年　無在不在　十方目前　極小同大
妄絶境界　極大同小　不見邊表　有即是無　無即是有
若不如是　必不須守　一即一切　一切即一　但能如是
何慮不畢　信心不二　不二信心　言語道斷　非去來今

Terms

thusness: 如是—*rushi* in Chinese and *nyoze* in Japanese, meaning "as it is," "things as they are." Also, suchness.

six-sense objects: The objects of seeing, hearing, smelling, tasting, touching, and thinking—namely, forms, sounds, odor, taste, touch, and phenomena.

Credit

Translated by Joan Halifax and the Editor.

SONG OF REALIZING THE WAY

Yongjia Xuanjiao (永嘉玄覺, d. 713), of the Tang Dynasty, wrote this long poem. Yongjia came from Yongjia Prefecture, in the Wen Region (present-day Zhejiang). After studying the Tiantai method of meditation, he studied Zen. Upon meeting and exchanging a few words with the Sixth Ancestor, Huineng, he received dharma transmission and stayed overnight at his community, so he was also called "Overnight Jiao." He went back to the Wen Region and taught.

The title of this poem is 證道歌—*Zhengdao Ge* in Chinese and *Shōdō Ka* in Japanese. The text is also included in the *Jingde Record of Transmission of the Lamp*.[37]

As this is a long verse, I have added section numbers for quick reference. Its ideographic version is

1

君不見

絕學無爲閒道人　不除妄想不求眞　無明實性即佛性
幻化空身即身　法身覺了無一物　本源自性天眞佛
五陰浮雲空去來　三毒水泡虚出沒　證實相無入法
刹那滅却阿鼻業　若將妄語誑衆生　自招拔舌塵沙劫
頓覺了如來禪　　六度萬行體中　圓夢裏明明有
六趣覺後空空　無大千　無罪福無損益
寂滅性中莫問覓　比來塵鏡未曾磨　今日分明須剖析
誰無念誰無生　若實無生無不　生喚取機關木人問
求佛施功早晚成

2

放四大莫把捉　寂滅性中隨飲啄　諸行無常一切空
即是如來大圓覺　決定説表眞僧　有人不肯任情徵

直截根源佛所印　摘葉尋枝我不能　摩尼珠人不識
如來藏裏親收得　六般神用空不空　一顆圓光色非色
淨五眼得五力　　唯證乃知難可測　鏡裏看形見不難
水中捉月爭拈得　常獨行常獨步　　達者同遊涅槃路
調古神清風自高　貌頦骨剛人不顧

3

窮釋子口稱貧　　實是身貧道不貧　貧則身常披縷褐
道則心藏無價珍　無價珍用無盡　　利物應機終不悋
三身四智體中圓　八解六通心地印　上士一決一切了
中下多聞多不信　但自懷中解垢衣　誰能向外誇精進
從他謗任他非　　把火燒天徒自疲　我聞恰似飲甘露
銷融頓入不思議　觀惡言是功德　　此即成吾善知識
不因訕謗起冤親　何表無生慈忍力　宗亦通說亦通
定慧圓明不滯空　非但我今獨達了　恒沙諸佛體皆同
師子吼無畏說　　百獸聞之皆腦裂　香象奔波失却威
天龍寂聽生欣悦　遊江海涉山川　　尋師訪道爲參禪
自從認得曹谿路　了知生死不相關　行亦禪坐亦禪語
默動靜體安然　　縱遇鋒刀常坦坦　假饒毒藥也閒閒
我師得見然燈佛　多劫曾爲忍辱仙　幾迴生幾迴死
生死悠悠無定止　自從頓悟了無生　於諸榮辱何憂喜
入深山住蘭若　　岑崟幽邃長松下　優游靜坐野僧家
閴寂安居實蕭灑

4

覺即了不施功　　一切有爲法不同　住相布施生天福
猶如仰箭射虛空　勢力盡箭還墜　　招得來生不如意
爭似無爲實相門　一超直入如來地　但得本莫愁末
如淨琉璃含寶月　既能解此如意珠　自利利他終不竭
江月照松風吹　　永夜清宵何所爲　佛性戒珠心地印
霧露雲霞體上衣　降龍鉢解虎錫　　兩鈷金環鳴歷歷
不是標形虛事持　如來寶杖親蹤跡

5

不求眞不斷妄　　了知二法空無相　　無相無空無不空
即是如來眞實相　　心鏡明鑒無礙　　廓然瑩徹周沙界
萬象森羅影現中　　一顆圓光非内外　　豁達空撥因果
莽莽蕩蕩招殃禍　　棄有著空病亦然　　還如避溺而投火
捨妄心取眞理　　取捨之心成巧偽　　學人不了用修行
深成認賊將爲子　　損法財滅功德　　莫不由斯心意識
是以禪門了却心　　頓入無生知見力

6

大丈夫秉慧劍　　般若鋒兮金剛焰　　非但空摧外道心
早曾落却天魔膽　　震法雷擊法鼓　　布慈雲兮灑甘露
龍象蹴踏潤無邊　　三乘五性皆醒悟　　雪山肥膩更無雜
純出醍醐我常納　　一性圓通一切性　　一法遍含一切法
一月普現一切水　　一切水月一月攝　　諸佛法身入我性
我性同共如來合　　一地具足一切地　　非色非心非行業
彈指圓成八萬門　　刹那滅却三祇劫　　一切數句非數句
與吾靈覺何交涉　　不可毀不可讚體　　若虛空勿涯岸
不離當處常湛然　　覓即知君不可見　　取不得捨不得
不可得中只麼得　　默時説説時默　　大施門開無壅塞
有問我解何宗　　報道摩訶般若力　　或是或非人不識
逆行順行天莫測　　吾早曾經多劫修　　不是等閒相誑惑

7

建法幢立宗旨　　明明佛勅曹溪是　　第一迦葉首傳燈
二十八代西天記　法東流入此土　　菩提達磨爲初祖
六代傳衣天下聞　　後人得道何窮數　　眞不立妄本空
有無俱遣不空空　二十空門元不著　　一性如來體自同
心是根法是塵　　兩種猶如鏡上痕　　痕垢盡除光始現
心法雙忘性即眞　　嗟末法惡時世　　衆生福薄難調制
去聖遠兮邪見深　　魔強法弱多恐害　　聞説如來頓教門
恨不滅除令瓦碎　　作在心殃在身　　不須冤訴更尤人

8

欲得不招無間業　莫謗如來正法輪　旃檀林無雜樹
欝密森沈師子住　境靜林間獨自遊　走獸飛禽皆遠去
師子兒衆隨後　三歲便能大哮吼　若是野干逐法王
百年妖怪虛開口　圓頓教勿人情　有疑不決直須爭
不是山僧逞人我　修行恐落斷常坑　非不非是不是
差之毫釐失千里　是則龍女頓成佛　非則善星生陷墜
吾早年來積學問　亦曾討疏尋經論　分別名相不知休
入海算沙徒自困　却被如來苦訶責　數他珍寶有何益
從來蹭蹬覺虛行　多年枉作風塵客

9

種性邪錯知解　不達如來圓頓制　二乘精進勿道心
外道明無智慧　亦愚癡亦小騃　空拳指上生實解
執指爲月枉施功　根境法中虛捏怪　不見一法即如來
方得名爲觀自在　了即業障本來空　未了應須還夙債
饑逢王膳不能飱　病遇醫王爭得瘥　在欲行禪知見力
火中生蓮終不壞　勇施犯重悟無生　早時成佛于今在
師子吼無畏説　深嗟懵頑皮靼鞋　知犯重障菩提
不見如來開祕訣　有二比丘犯婬殺　波離螢光增罪結
維摩大士頓除疑　猶如赫日銷霜雪　不思議解脱力
妙用恒沙也無極

10

四事供養敢辭勞　萬兩黃金亦銷得　粉骨碎身未足酬
一句了然超百億　法中王最高勝　恒沙如來同共證
我今解此如意珠　信受之者皆相應　了了見無一物
亦無人亦無佛　大千沙界海中漚　一切聖賢如電拂
假使鐵輪頂上旋　定慧圓明終不失　日可冷月可熱
衆魔不能壞眞説　象駕崢嶸謾進途　誰螳蜋能拒轍
大象不遊於兎徑　大悟不拘於小節　莫將管見謗蒼蒼
未了吾今爲君訣

Terms and Names

buddha nature: The capacity for becoming a buddha, which is inherent in all sentient beings according to Mahāyāna Buddhist teaching.

self nature: One's own inherent capacity.

three poisons: Greed, hatred, and ignorance.

five streams: See *five streams of body, mind, and heart* (p. 129).

Avīchi Hell: Sanskrit. Transliterated as 阿鼻 (*Abi*). Translated as 無間 (*mugen*), literally, "no interval." The hell of unceasing suffering; the worst of all hells.

Tathāgata: Sanskrit, literally, "one who has thus gone," "one who has thus come," or "one who has come from thusness." Honorific name for Shākyamuni Buddha, also indicating buddhas in general.

Tathāgata's Zen: Meditation taught by Shākyamuni Buddha, in contrast to "Ancestral Zen" taught by Bodhidharma and his dharma descendants.

six realizations: 六度—*liudu* in Chinese and *rokudo* in Japanese—is the six pāramitās. The basis for a bodhisattva's practice leading to the shore of nirvāna: giving, keeping precepts, patience, vigorous effort, meditation, and prajñā (wisdom beyond wisdom).

six paths: 六趣—*liuqu* in Chinese and *rokusho* in Japanese. See *six paths* (p. 157).

nirvāna: Sanskrit. Transliteration, 涅槃—*niepan* in Chinese and *nehan* in Japanese. The state of enlightenment attained by Shākyamuni Buddha, or by any other buddha. Literally, "extinction of fire," meaning extinction of desires or liberation from the cycle of birth, death, and rebirth. In Mahāyāna Buddhism, nirvāna is viewed as not separate from birth and death, as opposed to extinction of birth and death.

stained mirror: Hindrance to a round bronze mirror, which represents unmarred awakening.

four great elements: An ancient Indian classification: earth, water, fire, and air.

six miraculous powers: The celestial feet, the celestial eye, the celestial ear, seeing others' minds, knowing the past, and the power to be free from desire.

five eyes: Fleshly eyes, heavenly eyes, wisdom eyes, (bodhisattva's) dharma eyes, and buddha eyes.

five excellent powers: Trust, effort, mindfulness, samādhi, and wisdom.

three bodies: Threefold body of the Buddha. See p. 154.

four wisdoms: Four aspects of wisdom by one who has become free from delusion and attained the fruit of buddhahood: great round-mirror wisdom, equal-nature wisdom, wondrous-observation wisdom, and conducting-action wisdom.

eight liberations: Eight types of samādhi for becoming free from delusion and attaining liberation: concentrate on a certain object and become free from desire, concentrate on one point, separate the mind from outer objects, arrive at the pure state of body and mind, become free from distinguishing, arrive at a boundless stage, arrive at the source, and arrive at the stage where the source is always present in actuality.

samādhi: Sanskrit. Concentration: serene, settled, and collected state of body and mind in meditation.

Caoxi: A way to name the Sixth Chinese Ancestor, Dajian Huineng, as he taught at Baolin Monastery, Caoxi, Shao Region (present-day Guangdong).

Dīpankara Buddha: Literally, "solid light buddha," also called "Lamp Burning Tathāgata." A mystic buddha said to be the first one to give a prediction of enlightenment to a bodhisattva; one of the former lives of Shākyamuni Buddha.

Sorcerer of Patience: The name of Shākyamuni Buddha in one of his earlier lives practicing as a bodhisattva.

deva world: One of the six paths. See p. 157.

two-prong thunderbolt: Originally a pounder with sharp-pronged edges on both ends with a handle in the center. Later, a symbol of the Buddha's solid wisdom and crushing of delusions.

prajñā: See p. 9.

vajra: Diamond; also a two-, three-, or five-pronged thunderbolt. See above, *two-prong thunderbolt.*

Three Vehicles: According to the traditional Mahāyāna Buddhist view, the Buddha's teaching is classified in three ways: the *shrā-vaka* (listener) vehicle, the *pratyeka-buddha* (solitary awakened one) vehicle, and the Mahāyāna, or Great Vehicle. The first two are called in a derogatory way the "Hīnayāna," or Lesser (Small) Vehicle(s). They are also called the "Two Vehicles." The Great Vehicle, which emphasizes bringing all sentient beings to enlightenment, is also called the "Bodhisattva Vehicle."

five capacities: Five different capacities for enlightenment.

Snow Mountains: The Himālayas, described in sūtras as the place where Shākyamuni Buddha practiced in his former life.

eighty thousand gates: Eighty-four thousand is a commonly used number in Buddhism to indicate a great many aspects of teaching.

Mahākāshyapa: A senior disciple of Shākyamuni Buddha who was engaged in rigorous ascetic practice. Regarded as the First Ancestor of the Zen School.

twenty-eight generations: The early Indian ancestors of Zen—from Mahākāshyapa to Bodhidharma.

first six generations: The early Chinese ancestors from Bodhidharma to Huineng—the Sixth Ancestor.

twenty gates of emptiness: Eighteen gates of emptiness are explained in the *Mahā Prajñā Pāramitā Sūtra.* Sometimes two more gates are added.

Sunakshatra: A son of Shākyamuni Buddha. He was ordained but went back to lay life and slandered buddha dharma, which caused him to fall into Avīchi Hell.

Two Vehicles: See *Three Vehicles* (p. 173).

One Who Sees Freely: A name of Avalokiteshvara.

Medicine King: The Buddha who heals the delusion and ignorance of sentient beings.

Upāli: One of the ten disciples of Shākyamuni Buddha. Although coming from a low class, the Buddha ordained him earlier than those from a higher class, and put him in a senior position. The story of Upāli giving trivial advice to two monks who committed grave crimes, but being corrected by Vimalakīrti, is found in the *Vimalakīrti Sūtra.*

Vimalakīrti: An enlightened layman who is the main figure of the Mahāyāna's *Vimalakīrti Sūtra.*

billion worlds: A great number of worlds of phenomena.

CREDIT

Translated by Peter Levitt and the Editor.

BEING ONE AND MANY

Shitou Xiqian (石頭希遷, 700–790), of the Tang Dynasty, wrote this poem. He was ordained by the Sixth Chinese Ancestor, Huineng. After his master's death, Shitou studied with Qingyuan Xingsi and became his dharma heir. As he sat zazen continually in a hut built on a rock at Nan Monastery, Mount Heng (Hunan), he was called Priest "Rock Head" (Shitou). His posthumous name is Great Master Wuji.

This poem is frequently chanted in monasteries and groups of the Japanese Sōtō School. The title of this poem is 參同契—*Cantong Qi* in Chinese and *Sandō Kai* in Japanese. The text is also included in the *Jingde Record of Transmission of the Lamp.*[38]

Its ideographic version is

竺土大仙心　東西密相付　人根有利鈍　道無南北祖
靈源明皎潔　枝派暗流注　執事元是迷　契理亦非悟
門門一切境　迴互不迴互　迴而更相涉　不爾依位住
色本殊質象　聲元異樂苦　暗合上中言　明明清濁句
四大性自復　如子得其母　火熱風動搖　水濕地堅固
眼色耳音聲　鼻香舌鹹醋　然依一一法　依根葉分布
本末須歸宗　尊卑用其語　當明中有暗　勿以暗相遇
當暗中有明　勿以明相覩　明暗各相對　比如前後步
萬物自有功　當言用及處　事存函蓋合　理應箭鋒拄
承言須會宗　勿自立規矩　觸目不會道　運足焉知路
進步非近遠　迷隔山河固　謹白參玄人　光陰莫虛度

TERMS

Being One and Many: The ideographs for the title: *Can* means "three," and also means "many." *Tong* means "same," or in this case "one." *Qi* means "merge." Thus, the title indicates the interaction of the pluralistic and singularistic paradigms.

sage of India: Shākyamuni Buddha.

northern and southern ancestors: Soon before the time of Shitou, two streams of Zen were emerging: the first one, a group initiated by Yuquan Shenxiu, a dharma heir of the Fifth Ancestor, Daman Hongren. This group, emphasizing gradual enlightenment, was labeled as the "Northern School." Shenxiu's dharma brother, the Sixth Ancestor, Dajian Huineng, emphasized sudden enlightenment. His group was called the "Southern School," which became the main stream of Chinese Zen.

four elements: See p. 172.

CREDIT

Translated by Philip Whalen, Tom Cabarga, and the Editor. Revised by Joan Halifax and the Editor.

SONG OF THE GRASS HUT

Written also by Shitou Xiqian, the author of "Being One and Many," its title is 草庵歌—*Cao'an Ge* in Chinese and *Sōan Ka* in Japanese. This poem is not chanted as commonly as the above piece. Again, this text is included in the *Jingde Record of Transmission of the Lamp*.[39]

It ideographic version is

吾結草庵無寶貝	飯了從容圖睡快	成時初見茆草新
破後還將茆草蓋	住庵人鎮常在	不屬中間與內外
世人住處我不住	世人愛處我不愛	庵雖小含法界
方丈老人相體解	上乘菩薩信無疑	中下聞之必生怪
問此庵壞不壞	壞與不壞主元在	不居南北與東西
基上堅牢以為最	青松下明窓內	玉殿朱樓未為對
衲帔襟頭萬事休	此時山僧都不會	住此庵休作解
誰誇鋪席圖人買	迴光返照便歸來	廓達靈根非向背
遇祖師親訓誨	結草為庵莫生退	百年拋却任縱橫
擺手便行且無罪	千種言萬般解	只要教君長不昧
欲識庵中不死人	豈離而今遮皮袋	

TERMS
original master: One who is beyond time.
skin bag: A human being.

CREDIT
Translated by Taigen Dan Leighton and the Editor.

THE JEWEL MIRROR AWARENESS

Dongshan Liangji (洞山良价 807–869), of the Tang Dynasty, wrote this poem. Dongshan became a monk in childhood and then studied extensively with teachers, including Nanquan Puyuan and Guishan Lingyou. Later he became a dharma heir of the Yunyan Tansheng, Qingyuan Line, and taught at Mount Dong, in the Rui Region (present-day Jiangxi). He is regarded as a founder of the Caodong School, one of the Five Schools of Chinese Zen. His posthumous name is Great Master Wuben.

The title of this poem is 寶鏡三昧—*Baojing Sanmei* in Chinese and *Hōkyō Zammai* in Japanese. The Chinese text is in the *Taishō* canon.[40]

This text reflects the teaching of the "five ranks" or "five positions," the philosophical underpinning of Caodong practice. It is frequently chanted in monasteries and groups of the Japanese Sōtō School.

Its ideographic version is

如是之法	佛祖密付	汝今得之	宜善保護	銀盌盛雪	明月藏鷺
類之不齊	混則知處	意不在言	來機亦赴	動成窠臼	差落顧佇
背觸俱非	如大火聚	但形文彩	即屬染污	夜半正明	天曉不露
為物作則	用拔諸苦	雖非有為	不是無語	如臨寶鏡	形影相覩
汝不是渠	渠正是汝	如世嬰兒	五相完具	不去不來	不起不住
婆婆和和	有句無句	終不得物	語未正故	重離六爻	偏正回互
疊而為三	變盡成五	如荎草味	如金剛杵	正中妙挾	敲唱雙舉
通宗通途	挾帶挾路	錯然則吉	不可犯忤	天真而妙	不屬迷悟
因緣時節	寂然昭著	細入無間	大絕方所	毫忽之差	不應律呂
今有頓漸	緣立宗趣	宗趣分矣	即是規矩	宗通趣極	真常流注
外寂中搖	係駒伏鼠	先聖悲之	為法檀度	隨其顛倒	以緇為素
顛倒想滅	肯心自許	要合古轍	請觀前古	佛道垂成	十劫觀樹
如虎之缺	如馬之馵	以有下劣	寶几珍御	以有驚異	鼇奴白牯
羿以巧力	射中百步	箭鋒相值	巧力何預	木人方歌	石女起舞
非情識到	寧容思慮	臣奉於君	子順於父	不順非孝	不奉非輔
潛行密用	如愚如魯	但能相續	名主中主		

TERMS AND NAMES

awareness: Sanmei in the title of this poem is the Chinese transliteration of *samādhi* in Sanskrit, meaning "serene, settled, and
collected state of body and mind in meditation."

thusness: 如是—*rushi* in Chinese and *nyoze* in Japanese. See p. 166.

five aspects: 五相—*wuxiang* in Chinese and *gosō* in Japanese. Aspects
of action that are incomplete for an ordinary infant: rising, abiding, coming, going, and speaking.

double "fire" hexagram: The ancient Chinese philosophy of change
(易—*i* in Chinese and *eki* in Japanese) is known for its main
scripture *Ijing* (*I-ching*). According to its teaching, there are
eight basic situations—*qia, dui, li, zhen, xun, kan, gen,* and *kun,*
which correspond to heaven, lake, fire, thunder, ground, gorge,
bound, and field. Each of these situations is represented by a tri-
gram—a combination of three horizontal lines: solid, or broken
into two with space in between. For example, the third situation, *li* (離), is represented by a broken line stacked between solid
lines: ☲. A solid line is usually related to yang, and a broken line,
yin. But Dongshan relates the former to *zheng* (nonduality) and
the latter to *pian* (duality). (See the entry for *five,* below.) In the
philosophy of change, the eight situations are combined two-
fold, which makes sixty-four situations, represented by sixty-four
hexagrams that are trigrams stacked one top of another. One of
them, "double fire," is an intense situation of duality contained
within nonduality.

three: This may refer to Dongshan's "three phrases" for guiding students—a statement for going forward, a statement within the
gate, and one of going beyond ten billion.

five: This seems to refer to Dongshan's "five ranks" or "five positions"—a theory of understanding reality, which consists of two
elements: Chinese, *zheng,* 正 (*shō*) and *pian,* 偏 (*hen*). *Zheng*
represents nonduality and *pian* represents duality. Dongshan's

theory consists of (1) pian within zheng, (2) zheng within pian, (3) zheng alone, (4) pian alone, and (5) zheng and pian together.

within nonduality: See above.

five-flavored herb: 茎草—*zhicai* in Chinese and *chisō* in Japanese. Climbing *kadsura* or vine.

teachings of sudden and gradual: See *northern and southern ancestors*, p. 177.

Yi: A legendary archer who is said to have shot down nine suns, when ten suns emerged and caused people to suffer.

CREDIT

Translated by Philip Whalen, Tom Cabarga, and the Editor. Revised by Joan Halifax and the Editor.

THE POINT OF ZAZEN

Eihei Dōgen wrote this poem after the poem of the same title by Hongzhi Zhengju (宏智正覺, 1091–1157), of the Song Dynasty. Hongzhi had been a prominent Chinese master of the Caodong School—the lineage Dōgen inherited. Hongzhi advocated "Silent Illumination Zen." Dōgen adopted Hongzhi's verse, changing several words and making a stunning improvement.

Dōgen went to China to study Zen in 1223, was trained by Tiantong Rujing of the Tiantong Monastery (in present-day Zhejiang), and brought back his teaching to Japan in 1227. He established the Kōshō Hōrin Monastery in the south of the capital city, Kyōto, in 1233 and the Eihei Monastery in Echizen Province (present-day Fukui Prefecture) in 1246. He is regarded as the founder of the Sōtō School in Japan. *Treasury of the True Dharma Eye* (Shōbō Genzō)—a collection of over ninety essays—is his lifework. This poem, "The Point of Zazen," is part of the essay of the same title that he completed in 1242. Although this poem is not commonly chanted, it is a work that summarizes Dōgen's teaching on the essence of zazen—meditation in a sitting posture.

The title of this poem is 坐禅箴—*Zhuochan Zhen* in Chinese and *Zazen Shin* in Japanese.[41] Its original version in ideography is

佛佛要機	祖祖機要
不思量而現	不回互而成
不思量而現	其現自親
不回互而成	其成自證
其現自親	曾無染汚
其成自證	曾無正偏
曾無染汚之親	其親無委而脱落
曾無正偏之證	其證無圖而功夫
水清徹地兮	魚行似魚
空闊透天兮	鳥飛如鳥

TERMS

intimate: 親—*shin* in Japanese, literally meaning "parent," "close." Immediate experience. Close and inseparable.

dropping away: 脱落—*datsuraki* in Japanese. To experience complete freedom beyond delusion and enlightenment, with nonattachment to body and mind.

CREDIT

Translated by Philip Whalen and the Editor. Revised by Michael Wenger and the Editor.

IN PRAISE OF ZAZEN

Hakuin Ekaku (1685–1768), a Zen teacher, poet, calligrapher, and painter of the Edo Period, in Japan, wrote this poem.[42] Hakuin was ordained as a novice at the Shōin Monastery, a small Zen temple in

Suruga Province (present-day Shizuoka Prefecture) in 1699. After visiting a number of Zen masters, he practiced with Shōju Etan and had an enlightenment experience. In 1717 he became abbot of the Shōin Monastery. Many monks from all over Japan assembled and engaged in kōan studies with him. In 1761 he founded the Ryūtaku Monastery, also in Suruga Province. He is regarded as the restorer of the Rinzai School of Zen in Japan. This poem is chanted daily in Rinzai monasteries and groups.

The original Japanese title of this poem is 坐禪和讚—*Zazen Wasan*. As *wasan* means "praise in Japanese," this is written in a mixture of ideographs and phonetics:

衆生本来佛なり　　　　　水と氷の如くにて
水を離れて氷なく　　　　衆生の外に佛なし
衆生近きを知らずして　　遠く求むるはかなさよ
たとえば水の中に居て　　渇を叫ぶが如くなり
長者の家の子となりて　　貧里に迷うに異ならず
六趣輪廻の因縁は　　　　己が愚痴の闇路なり
闇路に闇路を踏そえて　　いつか生死を離るべき

夫れ摩訶衍の禪定は　　　稱歎するに餘りあり
布施や持戒の諸波羅蜜　　念佛懺悔修行等
そのしな多き諸善行　　　皆この中に歸するなり
一坐の功をなす人も　　　積し無量の罪ほろぶ
悪趣何處にありぬべき　　淨土即ち遠からず
かたじけなくもこの法を　一たび耳にふるる時
讚歎随喜する人は　　　　福を得る事限りなし

況や自ら回向して　　　　直に自性を證すれば
自性即ち無性にて　　　　既に戯論を離れたり
因果一如の門ひらけ　　　無二無三の道直し
無相の相を相として　　　行くも歸るも餘所ならず

無念の念を念として　　うたうも舞うも法の聲
三昧無礙の空ひろく　　四智圓明の月さえん
この時何をか求むべき　　寂滅現前するゆえに
當所即ち蓮華國　　この身即ち佛なり

TERMS AND NAMES

six realms: See *six paths,* p. 157.

other realizations: The six pāramitās—the basis for a bodhisattva's practice leading to the shore of nirvāna are: giving, keeping precepts, patience, vigorous effort, meditation, and prajñā.

four wisdoms: See p. 172.

CREDIT

Translated by the Editor.

PROSE CHANTS FOR STUDY

RECOMMENDING ZAZEN TO ALL PEOPLE

AFTER RETURNING to Japan from China in 1227, Dōgen wrote this proclamation in Chinese. It summarizes his intention to establish a single practice of Zen meditation in Japan; thus this has become one of the most revered texts in the Sōtō School. It is sometimes chanted and often studied in Sōtō monasteries and groups. The original manuscript, edited and handwritten by him in 1233, still exists. We present this later version. The original title for this text is 普勧坐禅儀—*Fukan Zazen Gi.*[43]

NAMES
Jeta Grove: "Garden of Solitude": in the south of the city of Shravasti, in Kōshala Kingdom, in central northern India. According to sūtras, this is where Shākyamuni Buddha's community practiced together in the monastery during the rainy season.

Shaolin Temple: Situated on Mount Song (in Henan), China, where Bodhidharma sat facing the wall for nine years.

CREDIT
Translated by Edward Brown and the Editor.

ON THE ENDEAVOR OF THE WAY

Dōgen wrote this essay in 1231 before he established his first monastery, Kōshō Hōrin. "On the Endeavor of the Way" is Dōgen's systematic elucidation of his understanding of Zen, based on the principle that practice and enlightenment are inseparable. This text reflects Dōgen's first attempt to express his thinking in the vernacular Japanese language. Until then Buddhist teachings had been studied and written almost exclusively in the Japanese form of Chinese.

This text is highly respected in the Sōtō School as Dōgen's most comprehensive explanation of dharma. However, Dōgen did not include the words "Treasury of the True Dharma Eye" at the beginning of its title. When he later edited the *Treasury of the True Dharma Eye,* he did not include this fascicle in either the seventy-five-fascicle or the twelve-fascicle version. The reason why Dōgen set aside this text may be that, since it was addressed to an open audience, it reflects his intention to spread dharma broadly, while his teaching evolved toward training a small number of committed students as his community matured.

According to Menzan Zuihō's *Eliminating Wrong Views on the Treasury of the True Dharma Eye* (Shōbō Genzō Byakujaku Ketsu, 1738), this text was discovered in a courtier's house in Kyōto. The original title for this text is 辨道話—*Bendō Wa.*[44]

"On the Endeavor of the Way" includes in its latter half a set of imaginary questions and answers where Dōgen responds to doubts and skepticism by those accustomed to conventional Buddhist practices. But here we present only the first half, which is the main part of the text, and is sometimes chanted in various Sōtō Zen centers.

TERMS AND NAMES

Myōzen: Butsuju Myōzen, 佛樹明全 (1184–1225, Japan). Dharma heir of Myōan Eisai. As abbot of the Kennin Monastery, Kyōto, he taught Rinzai Zen to Dōgen. He took Dōgen to China but died at the Tiantong Monastery during his stay.

Rinzai: Rinzai School. Japanese form of the Linji School. One of the two major schools of Japanese Zen Buddhism. Myōan Eisai is regarded as the founder.

Kennin Monastery: Zen monastery in Kyōto, founded by Myōan Eisai in 1203.

Eisai: Myōan Eisai (1141–1225, Japan). Went to China in 1168 and brought back Tiantai texts. Made a second visit to China between 1185 and 1191 to study Zen. Dharma heir of Xu'an Huaichang, of the Linji School. Author of *On Raising Zen and Protecting the Nation* (Kōzen Gokoku Ron). Founded Jufuku Monastery in Kamakura and Kennin Monastery in Kyōto. Regarded as founder of the Rinzai School, the Japanese form of the Linji School.

Zhe River: River that runs through Zhejiang Province, where the Five Mountains, the most important Zen monasteries, were located.

Five Gates: The major schools of Zen Buddhism established after the late Tang Dynasty China: Fayan, Guiyang, Caodong, Yunmen, and Linji Schools.

Rujing: Tiantong Rujing 天童如淨 (1163–1228, China). Dharma heir of Xuedou Zhijian, of the Caodong School. Between 1210 and 1225, he was successively abbot of Qingliang Monastery, in the Jiankang Region (Jiangsu); Ruiyan Monastery, in the Tai Region (Zhejiang); and Jingci Monastery, in the Hang Region (Zhejiang). In 1225 he became abbot of the Jingde Monastery, on Mount Tiantong, in the Ming Region (Zhejiang), where he transmitted dharma to Dōgen.

CREDIT

Translated by Lewis Richmond and the Editor.

ACTUALIZING THE FUNDAMENTAL POINT

Dōgen gave this text to his lay student Kōshū Yō on the full moon day of the eighth month of 1233. The first practice period Dōgen led ended at his training center—Kōshō Hōrin Monastery—on the full moon day (the fifteenth), the seventh month of that year. Kōshū must have joined the practice period, and perhaps he was leaving for his home on the southwestern island of Kyūshū.

The original Japanese title of this text is 現成公案—*Genjō Kōan.*[45] *Kōan*—the original word for "fundamental point" in the title—usually means an exemplary Zen story given by a teacher to a student for spiritual investigation. But Dōgen used the word here to point to the reality of all things.

"Actualizing the Fundamental Point" is probably the best known and most studied text of all Dōgen's writings, both for its summary of his teaching and for its poetic beauty. While other fascicles are focused on the themes indicated by their titles, "Actualizing the Fundamental Point" covers multiple themes, including awakened ones and nonawakened ones, enlightenment and delusion, birth and death, the potential of enlightenment (buddha nature) and the actualization of it. This text is sometimes chanted and often studied in Sōtō Zen groups.

NAMES

Mayu: Mayu Baoche (麻谷寶徹, ca. eighth century, China). Dharma heir of Mazu Daoyi, Nanyue Line. Taught at Mount Mayu, Pu Region (Shanxi).

CREDIT

Translated by Robert Aitken and the Editor. Revised at the San Francisco Zen Center and, later, at the Berkeley Zen Center.

NOTES

1. Daisetz Teitaro Suzuki, *An Introduction to Zen Buddhism* (London: Rider, 1957), 74.
2. Kazuaki Tanahashi, ed., *Treasury of the True Dharma Eye: Zen Master Dogen's Shobo Genzo* (Boston: Shambhala Publications, 2010), 332.
3. Learning about an unknown ideograph on the Internet: If you have only a printed or written version of the ideograph, go to www.nciku.com, draw the unknown ideograph with your mouse or trackpad in the *enter character* window and click *look up*. Then select the likely ideograph. Then, go to www.wiktionary.org. Paste the ideograph you have copied into the search box. Click the arrow. You will get much information on the ideograph, including its meanings, pronunciations, etymology, radical, and, in some cases, stroke order. These are just examples. There are many online dictionaries that work in a simlar way.
4. Kazuaki Tanahashi, *The Heart Sutra: A Comprehensive Guide to the Classic in Mahayana Buddhism* (Boston: Shambhala Publications, 2014), 73.
5. Tanahashi, *Treasury of the True Dharma Eye,* 332.
6. Ensemble Polyfoon, *Sandokai,* Ensemble Polyfoon, DVD, 2011.
7. *Taishō Shinshū Daizōkyō (Taishō),* no. 223, 8–223a.
8. Thich Nhat Hanh, *The Heart of Understanding: Commentaries on the Prajnaparamita Heart Sutra,* ed. Peter Levitt (Berkeley, CA: Parallax Press, 1988), 50.
9. *Taishō,* 40–84b.
10. Taigen Daniel Leighton and Shohaku Okumura, trans., *Dōgen's Pure Standards for the Zen Community* (Albany: State University of New York Press, 1996) 92.
11. Tanahashi, *Treasury of the True Dharma Eye,* 134.
12. Dawn Neal. "Confluence: Adoption & Adaptation of Loving-Kindness and Compassion Practice in Buddhist and Secular Contexts." Forthcoming, *Dharma Drum Journal,* 2015.
13. *Taishō,* no. 1060.
14. Shūyo Takubo. I also owe much to the scholarship of Shungen Kimura and Chitai Takenaka in their *Zenshū no Darani* (Dharanīs of the Zen Schools) (Tokyo: Daitō Shuppansha, 1998).
15. D. T. Suzuki, *Manual of Zen Buddhism* (London: Rider and Company, 1950), 23.

16. *Taishō,* no. 2087, 2–11, 932.
17. *Taishō,* no. 257.
18. Takubo, ibid., 123. Translation by Jan Chozen Bays and the Editor, and revised by Joan Halifax. Also, Kimura and Takenaka, *Zenshū no Darani,* 116.
19. Grace Schireson, *Zen Women: Beyond Tea Ladies, Iron Maidens, and Macho Masters* (Somerville, Mass.: 2009), 259.
20. *Taishō,* no. 278.
21. *Plum Village Chanting and Recitation Book* (Berkeley, CA: Parallax Press, 2000), 12.
22. *Taishō,* no. 2607, 82–771a.
23. *Zoku Zōkyō,* 2-16-5.
24. Leighton and Okumura, *Dōgen's Pure Standards,* 89.
25. Tanahashi, *Treasury of the True Dharma Eye,* 732.
26. *Taishō,* no. 374, 12–46. *Daihatsu Nehan Gyo* (Great Pari-nirvana Sutra), chap. 16.
27. *Zen'en Shingi,* 9. *Complete Writings of the Sōtō School* (Sōtōshu Zensho), 4–918. (Tokyo: Sōtōshu Zensho Kankokai, 1931), 9–918.
28. T. Griffith Foulk, trans., *Standard Observances of the Soto Zen School* (Tokyo: The Administrative Headquarters of Sōtō Zen Buddhism, 2010), 1–207.
29. *Taishō,* no. 2607, 82–771a.
30. This reading of the mantra is based on a description in Kimura and Takenaka, *Zenshu no Darani,* 103.
31. Sōtōshū Zensho Kankokai, *Sōtōshū Zensho* (Complete Writings of the Sōtō School) (Tokyo: Sōtōshū Zensho Kankokai, 1931), 4–918.
32. *Taishō,* no. 85.
33. Tanahashi, *Treasury of the True Dharma Eye,* 95.
34. Ibid., 889.
35. Zenshū Hōkan.
36. *Taishō,* no. 2076, 48–376b.
37. *Taishō,* no. 2014, 48–395c.
38. *Taishō,* no. 1986, 47–515a.
39. *Taishō,* no. 2076, 48–461c.
40. *Taishō,* no. 2076, 48-459b.
41. Tanahashi, *Treasury of the True Dharma Eye,* 303.
42. Shōkō Yoshizawa, ed., *Hakuin Zenji Hōgo Shū,* (Kyoto: Zen Bunka Kenkyu Kai, 2002), 13–263.
43. Ibid., 906.
44. Ibid., 3.
45. Ibid., 29.

SELECTED BIBLIOGRAPHY

Aitken, Robert. *Taking the Path of Zen.* San Francisco: North Point Press, 1982.

Anderson, Reb. *Being Upright: Zen Meditation and the Bodhisattva Precepts.* Berkeley, CA: Rodmell Press, 1999.

Coupey, Philippe, ed. *Sit: Zen Teachings of Master Taisen Deshimaru.* Prescott, AZ: Hohm Press, 1996.

Foster, Nelson. *The Roaring Stream: A New Zen Reader.* New York: The Ecco Press, 1996.

Foulk T. Griffith, trans. *Standard Observances of the Soto Zen School.* Tokyo: The Administrative Headquarters of Sōtō Zen Buddhism, 2010.

Glassman, Bernie. *Infinite Circle: Teachings in Zen.* Boston: Shambhala Publications, 2003.

Heine, Steven and Wright, Dale S., eds. *Zen Ritual: Studies of Zen Buddhist Theory in Practice.* Oxford and New York: Oxford University Press, 2008.

Kennett, Jiyu. *Selling Water by the River.* New York: Pantheon Books, 1972.

Leggett, Trevor. *A First Zen Reader.* Rutland, VT and Tokyo: Charles E. Tuttle Company, 1960.

Loori, John Daido. *The Eight Gates of Zen: Spiritual Training in an American Zen Monastery.* Mt. Tremper, NY: Dharma Communications, 1992.

Loori, John Daido. *The Eight Gates of Zen: A Program of Zen Training.* Boston: Shambhala Publications, 2002.

Phillips, Bernard, ed. *The Essentials of Zen Buddhism.* London: Rider & Company, 1963.

Suzuki, Shunryu. *Branching Streams Flow in the Darkness: Zen Talks on the Sandokai.* Oakland, CA: University of California Press, 2001.

Tanahashi, Kazuaki. *The Heart Sutra: A Comprehensive Guide to the Classic of Mahayana Buddhism.* Boston: Shambhala Publications, 2014.